Puzzlesnacks

Puzzlesnacks

More Than 100 Clever, Bite-Size Puzzles for Every Solver

Eric Berlin

TILLER
PRESS

TILLER
PRESS

An Imprint of Simon & Schuster, Inc.
1230 Avenue of the Americas
New York, NY 10020

First Tiller Press trade paperback edition July 2019

TILLER PRESS and colophon are trademarks of Simon & Schuster, Inc.

For information about special discounts for bulk purchases, please contact Simon & Schuster Special Sales at 1-866-506-1949 or business@simonandschuster.com

The Simon & Schuster Speakers Bureau can bring authors to your live event. For more information or to book an event, contact the Simon & Schuster Speakers Bureau at 1-866-248-3049 or visit our website at www.simonspeakers.com.

Manufactured in the United States of America

3   5   7   9   10   8   6   4   2

ISBN 978-1-9821-3156-2
ISBN 978-1-9821-3157-9 (ebook)

Contents

Introduction

It all started with my daughter. She was a homeschooled kid for a while, and as part of that, I thought it might be a good idea to solve the *New York Times* crossword puzzle with her. You may know that the *New York Times* crossword starts off pretty easy on Monday, and becomes progressively more difficult through the week, concluding with a killer-diller of a puzzle on Saturday. My plan, perhaps obviously, was to stick to the easy Monday puzzles when working with my then-11-year-old.

There was a problem, though. Even an easy Monday crossword expects you to know things that a lot of people—especially 11-year-old kids—don't have in the easy-access part of their brains. Airport codes. Words in languages the solver does not speak. Actors and actresses of bygone eras. And a thousand other things that crossword regulars (like me) have long grown used to, but which can only serve to frustrate newcomers to the wonderful world of puzzles.

What the world needs, I thought, are puzzles that rely exclusively on words that people use every day. Get rid of the odd abbreviations and scientific terminology. Get rid of athletes

and singers unless they are truly household names. That still leaves *plenty* of words to work with. Also, I would make my puzzles a bit smaller in size. A typical daily newspaper crossword has 78 words. My puzzles would have between 16 and 30 words, to make them that much easier to solve in a single sitting.

And one more thing: The world of puzzles goes way, way, *way* beyond crosswords. Clever puzzlemakers over the years have devised dozens if not hundreds of fascinating ways to weave words together. I took some of the best puzzle types, shrunk them down a bit, and made them my own. But I owe a world of thanks to the constructors who came up with those puzzle types in the first place—innovators like Patrick Berry, Mike Shenk, and Will Shortz. They have my eternal gratitude.

When I first started making my small, friendly puzzles, I figured my audience would be kids like my daughter—bright, curious children looking for a fun way to exercise their brains. And while my puzzles were indeed sent out to thousands of kids around the world, I also noticed a funny thing happening: I used to ask my subscribers if they were parents, or teachers, or kids. If you were a kid, I would then ask for your age. A small but significant number of people would say to me, "I'm a kid. I'm a 43-year-old kid."

So here we are. I no longer make puzzles only for kids. I make puzzles for anybody who wants a small but pleasant challenge, using words you almost certainly know or, if not, can figure out without too much fuss.

After all, sometimes you don't want a big, heavy meal—you just want an enjoyable little bite. And sometimes you don't want a killer-diller puzzle that will take you three hours to solve . . . if you can manage to solve it at all. There are times when you simply want a snack. A Puzzlesnack!

I hope you find the snacks in these pages yummy and satisfying.

Take a Hint

These puzzles may use a straightforward vocabulary, but that doesn't mean you won't find some twists in the pages ahead. In some puzzles, you might know the answer to a particular clue . . . but you won't know where in the grid the answer is supposed to go. That's something you'll have to figure out. In other puzzles, some words need to be entered backward—but again, which ones? Oh, yes; there are plenty of curveballs waiting for you in these puzzles.

Never fear! If you find yourself getting a bit stuck, just look at the bottom of the page you're on. There you'll find several numbers. Each of these represents a hint at the back of the book. Take one of the numbers, look it up in the hint section (starting on page 115), and hopefully that will get you back on track.

Good luck and happy solving!

Puzzles

SOMETHING TO START YOU OFF

First, answer as many clues as you can. Each answer on the left side can be matched up to an answer on the right, via a rule that you'll have to determine. When you've paired up two words, carefully draw a straight line connecting the dot of one clue to the dot of the other. You will cross off some of the letters. After you've matched up all the words, the remaining letters, reading down, will describe you as a solver. *Answers, page 127.*

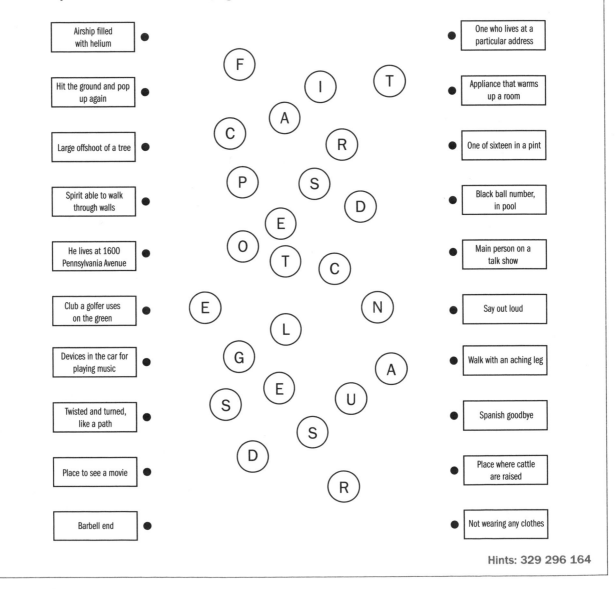

Airship filled with helium

Hit the ground and pop up again

Large offshoot of a tree

Spirit able to walk through walls

He lives at 1600 Pennsylvania Avenue

Club a golfer uses on the green

Devices in the car for playing music

Twisted and turned, like a path

Place to see a movie

Barbell end

One who lives at a particular address

Appliance that warms up a room

One of sixteen in a pint

Black ball number, in pool

Main person on a talk show

Say out loud

Walk with an aching leg

Spanish goodbye

Place where cattle are raised

Not wearing any clothes

Hints: 329 296 164

FLOWER POWER

Twelve answers in this flower-shaped grid will be entered clockwise, beginning from each numbered space and curving inward to the center. The other twelve answers will be entered counterclockwise, beginning from those same spaces. Work back and forth until you have completed the grid. *Answers, page 127.*

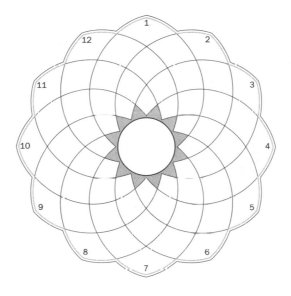

Clockwise
1 Level of a tall building
2 Name of the "Little Mermaid"
3 Fairy ___ (bedtime reading, perhaps)
4 Easy to lift
5 Shows extreme anger
6 Itsy-___
7 Device on a deli counter
8 Green shade
9 Layers of paint
10 Aspirin, cough syrup, etc.
11 Manmade water passage
12 Ledges next to windows

Counterclockwise
1 Performs in the chorus
2 Reference book for map lovers
3 Monster under a bridge, in folklore
4 Animals' homes
5 Girl in *Inside Out*
6 Alternative to a roll
7 Long, sad breaths
8 Group of eight
9 Roomful of students
10 Lace decoration on a table
11 Really, really want
12 Fry quickly on the stovetop

Hints: 24 175 36

AROUND THE BEND

Each answer in this puzzle starts in the appropriately numbered square . . . but when you run out of room in that row, you'll follow the arrow and write the rest of the answer backward in the next row down. This will then be the start of the next answer on the list. For example, the last three letters of PLAID in the small grid to the right become the first three letters of the next answer, DIARY. The grid below forms a loop—the first and last rows will be the same. *Answers, page 127.*

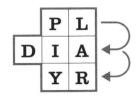

1   Capital of France
2   Loud part of a police car
3   "Not in a million years!"
4   Go over again, as schoolwork
5   Bizarro
6   Wearing clothes
7   Treats after dinner
8   Play a guitar, perhaps
9   Relative of a clam
10 Teacher's daily work
11 "Impossible!" (2 words)
12 Expressed boredom, maybe
13 Blue jeans material
14 Digger for diamonds
15 Give a new title
16 Send a message to online
17 Really, really angry
18 Opposite of multiplication
19 Louder (than)
20 Cut and gather, as a crop

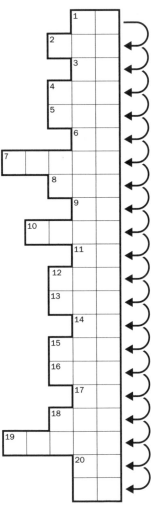

Hints: 294 237

ALPHABET SOUP

You can place one letter in each gray square to make a word of at least six letters reading across. Each letter of the alphabet will be used exactly once. Some of the letters in each row will not be used in that row's word. For example, in the first row you can place the letter R to make the word CARAMEL. Can you find the other 25 words? Some letters can go in more than one space, but there's only one way to place all of the letters. *Answers, page 128.*

ABCDEFGHIJKLMNOPQ~~R~~STUVWXYZ

T	O	S	C	A	**R**	A	M	E	L	T
A	S	A	N	D		I	C	H	O	N
R	A	M	A	N		I	O	N	E	D
C	R	I	M	I		A	L	T	E	R
G	R	A	S	P		R	I	N	K	S
P	S	E	N	T		N	C	E	L	H
A	T	H	I	C		U	P	L	A	N
S	H	O	R	E		E	R	E	E	L
A	S	H	A	R		O	N	I	C	A
C	A	N	D	R		I	D	I	A	N
A	G	G	R	A		I	T	Y	O	R
P	E	D	E	S		A	L	C	E	D
S	P	A	I	N		U	R	Y	A	L
A	R	B	O	U		U	E	T	I	C
D	E	N	C	A		B	A	G	E	L
O	S	E	L	T		E	R	E	B	S
B	O	H	U	N		R	E	D	I	N
P	R	E	L	A		E	S	H	A	R
B	U	N	C	H		R	I	S	M	A
S	T	A	U	T		O	R	M	O	D
T	U	N	I	C		C	L	E	N	Y
D	A	N	S	A		M	O	N	T	H
S	T	R	A	M		O	L	I	N	E
C	H	O	R	I		A	M	I	S	T
S	C	O	S	T		M	E	A	N	T
P	O	L	A	W		W	A	R	D	Y

Hints: 202 287

HEXED

Each six-letter answer in this puzzle will be entered around its number, starting in the space with the arrow and proceeding in the direction the arrow points (like SAMPLE in the example to the right). As extra assistance, the top row of hexes and the bottom row of hexes will have the same letters in the same order. *Answers, page 128.*

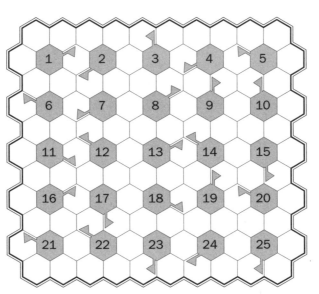

1 Smelly food disliked by vampires
2 Using oars, in a boat
3 Number of fingers on four hands
4 Halloween goodies
5 Stuns
6 Large building where airplanes are stored
7 Pained sounds
8 Make tidier, with "up"
9 Falcon's claws
10 Percussion instrument sort of like a large rattle
11 Trapped
12 Copperheads, diamondbacks, etc.
13 One half of Congress
14 Music from the 1950s, for example

15 Emmys and Grammys
16 Depended (upon)
17 They like to walk in the woods
18 Really smart person
19 Animated film featuring a saber-toothed squirrel (2 words)
20 Dances in a line
21 Coin featuring Thomas Jefferson
22 Get smaller
23 Dependable
24 Say a second time
25 Answer to the riddle "What is full of holes but can hold water?"

Hints: 52 34 146

SPIRAL

In this puzzle, one set of words will start at the 1 and spiral its way inward to the 50. Another set of words will start at the 50 and wind its way outward, back to the 1. Work back and forth between the two lists of clues until you have the whole spiral filled. *Answers, page 128.*

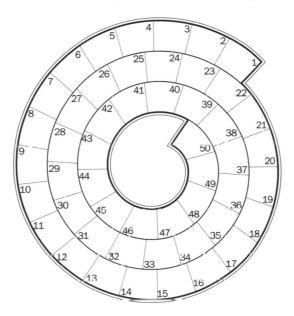

Inward

1–4: Kill, as a monster
5–11: Herb used on pizza
12–17: Plants in your backyard
18–24: Filled with strong emotions
25–29: Device that connects a computer to the Internet
30–37: Requirement for some Web sites
38–42: Spaghetti, tortellini, etc.
43–47: US president #44
48–50: Quick little snooze

Outward

50–45: Central American country known for its canal
44–40: Vessels on the sea
39–34: Tarzan, for one
33–28: Continue after stopping for a while
27–23: Some sports stadiums (notably those that can be used in any type of weather)
22–20: Butterfly catcher's aid
19–16: Baseball team count
15–10: Fire-breathing monster
9–7: What the number of candles on a cake represents
6–1: Kansas City's baseball team

Hints: 311 278

ZEBRA CROSSING

Answer words go across the three rows, clued in order—you'll write one letter in each triangle. Another set of answers will go diagonally down the zebra stripes. There is one set of clues for the white stripes and another set of clues for the gray stripes, but you will need to figure out which answer goes where. *Answers, page 128.*

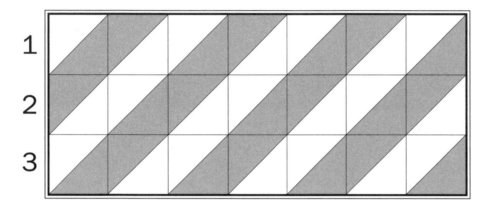

Rows

1. "Knuckle sandwich"
   Unable to ride certain
   amusement-park rides
   Measurement used
   for plots of land
2. Took a risk
   Stovetop items
   Hairdresser's location
3. Say grace, for example
   Had in one's hands
   Inventor of the lightbulb

White Stripes

▶ Athlete's reward, often
▶ Shoulder bag part
▶ Denials of permission
▶ Wiped away
▶ The worst possible grade

Gray Stripes

▶ "That's bad news!"
   (2 words)
▶ King's home
▶ Uppermost letter on a
   compass
▶ Andy's *Toy Story* neighbor
▶ Neither gas nor liquid

Hints: 315 133 241 111

GOTTA SPLIT

The clues in this puzzle have split! The list on the left shows the first half of every clue. The list on the right shows all of the second halves. Figure out which halves go together. When you've properly put together a clue, add up the numbers in each part. The sum matches a number in the grid, which is where the answer should be placed. *Answers, page 128.*

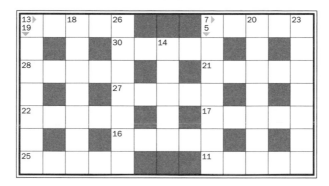

	First Half		Second Half
1	Like an unsharpened	1	Under
2	Two times	2	Of the present day
3	Horse's	3	Two of them
4	Directly	4	Love
5	Baseball catchers	5	With your shoulders
6	Divine creature	6	Pencil
7	Police officer's	7	Wyoming
8	Many camels have	8	Wear them on their hands
9	Say "I don't know"	9	Tops (hyph.)
10	Lady's	10	A stage
11	Office device that	11	All in black
12	State north of	12	Senses
13	French word for	13	Outfit
14	Thin cotton	14	Four
15	Man on	15	Fastens papers together
16	Evening	16	Wearing a halo
17	Warrior dressed	17	Carryall
18	One of the five	18	Sound

Hints: 75 138 215

ONE TWO THREE

This is a regular crossword puzzle except for one small thing: Each box will receive one, two, or three letters. The answer to 1-Across has been written in, as an example and to get you started. *Answers, page 129.*

Across

1 Story told in song
4 Tank engine of children's TV
7 Game where prizes are won if you choose the right numbers
8 Come up with, as a new idea
9 Small trumpet without valves
11 No longer afloat
12 Tiny insect that feeds on the sap of plants
14 One of the primary colors
15 Having to do with the moon
16 At the front of the line, say
18 Nutritious green vegetable
20 Make larger in number
23 Outer limits
24 *Star ____*

Down

1 Ink stain
2 Change, as a dress's length
3 Insect that's often red with black spots
4 Use your brain
5 Kitchen sight
6 Place for a sailboat's sail
10 It has 366 days
11 Start of the evening
13 Small rise in the landscape
15 Midday meals
17 No longer alive, as a species
18 Kept secretive watch (on)
19 Pester to get something done
21 Back end
22 Look for something that's hidden

Hints: 134 54 28

HALF AND HALF

In this puzzle, you'll spell a series of six-letter words, with half the letters in one box and half in another. Each pair of boxes connected by a line will spell the word clued by that line's number. All words read from left to right. The first and last boxes in the chain will contain the same letters, as with MANTLE, BATTLE, and BATMAN in the example to the right. *Answers, page 129.*

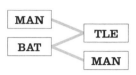

1 Destructive chaos
2 "The Star Spangled Banner," for example
3 Branched horn on a moose
4 Having more height
5 Ability, such as for singing or dancing
6 Mother or father
7 Sitting room
8 One who works at sea
9 Extremely good people
10 Dangerous shots to film, in the movies
11 What's left after trees are chopped down
12 Big winners, at the end of a tournament
13 "Take a ____!" ("I dare you!")
14 Hypnotic state
15 Sets of railway cars
16 Red-breasted birds
17 Thief
18 Person who cuts hair
19 Purple dinosaur of children's TV
20 Company behind *Frozen*
21 Anxious or alarmed state

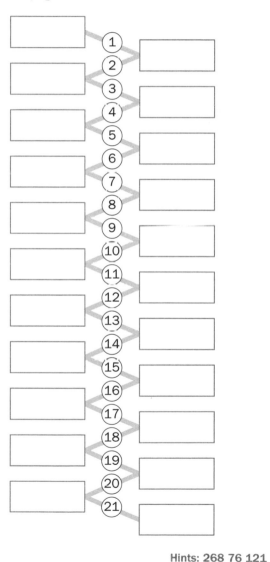

Hints: 268 76 121

MENTAL BLOCKS

In each puzzle below, the letters in the given three-letter word can be used in all of the blank blocks to form seven words reading across. Each of the three letters will be used at least once in each word. Clues are given for the seven words, but not in order. *Answers, page 129.*

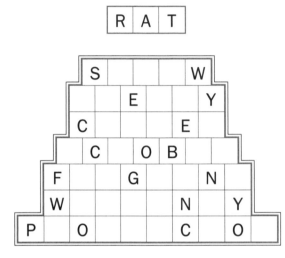

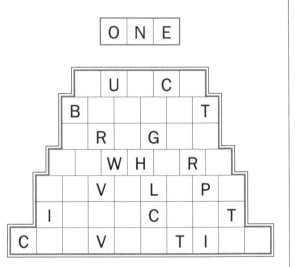

- Agreement that you can return something you've purchased if it breaks
- Device useful for measuring angles
- Giving off a strong odor, as a flower
- Gymnast in the circus
- Hole made by the impact of a meteor
- Material used by one of the Three Little Pigs
- Peace-making agreement between warring countries

- 1/16th of a pound
- Large, multiday gathering of people with a similar interest
- Letter container
- Neighbor of Washington and Idaho
- Not guilty of a crime
- Not in any place
- Woman's fanciful hat that's fastened under the chin with strings

Hints: 123 312 81 219

YOU CAN QUOTE ME

Write the answer to each clue on the dashes, and then transfer each letter to its correspondingly numbered square in the grid to spell out a quotation from Groucho Marx. Words in the quote that don't end on one line will continue on the next. Black squares separate the words of the quote. As you fill in letters in the quote, try to figure out some of its words—doing so will in turn help you with the answers to the clues. An extra bit of assistance: The dozen answers below are in alphabetical order. *Answers, page 129.*

1B		2F	3K	4H	5C		6I	7A	8G	9K	10J	11H	12E	13J	14C	15F		16A	17L
18C	19G		20E	21F	22I	23C	24G	25J	26L	27F	28A			29D	30G	31H	32B	33F	
34H	35A	36C	37H		38I	39F	40H	41G	42B	43C	44H	45E		46B	47D	48E	49J	50L	
51C	52H		53K	54G	55E		56B	57K	58G		59F		60F	61J		62F	63K	64C	
65J		66K	67A	68G		69E	70I	71K	72B	73D		74F	75C	76I		77G		78J	79A	80C
	81K	82E	83G	84F		85A		86A	87D	88H	89B								

A. Listening to your parents, showing good manners, and so on
__ __ __ __ __ __ __ __
86 7 67 85 16 35 79 28

B. Cut of meat often used in pot roast
__ __ __ __ __ __ __
42 32 1 56 89 72 46

C. Masked arch-enemy of the Fantastic Four (2 words)
__ __ __ __ __ __ __ __ __ __
5 51 23 64 14 18 80 75 43 36

D. Unit of currency in France, Germany, Spain, etc.
__ __ __ __
29 47 73 87

E. An ugly building in a nice neighborhood, for example
__ __ __ __ __ __ __
20 45 55 12 69 48 82

F. 2016 Pixar sequel (2 words)
__ __ __ __ __ __ __ __ __ __ __
2 59 15 21 62 27 60 84 39 74 33

G. Music genre known for loud electric guitars (2 words)
__ __ __ __ __ __ __ __ __ __
54 68 24 30 19 77 41 58 83 8

H. Briefly spoke of
__ __ __ __ __ __ __ __ __
40 31 4 34 11 88 52 37 44

I. There are 54 of them in a nine-inning baseball game
__ __ __ __
76 22 70 38

J. Standing ___ (what every performer hopes for)
__ __ __ __ __ __ __
65 10 78 25 13 61 49

K. Number in a baker's dozen
__ __ __ __ __ __ __ __
66 71 3 81 53 9 57 63

L. Neckwear for men
__ __ __ __
6 26 17 50

Hints: 165 19 98

PACKING CRATES

Two words will go in each row of this grid, clued in order. Another set of words can be found in the fifteen "Crates," always reading row by row, as demonstrated by the examples to the right. Can you pack the crates with all the right answers? *Answers, page 130.*

S	A
M	P
L	E

S	A	M
P	L	E

Rows

1   Costumed supporter of a sports team
Word following a prayer

2   Hardly ever seen
Member of the choir

3   Part of many a superhero's outfit
Unwilling to part with money

4   "Grand" musical instrument
____ Day (September holiday)

5   ___-free (like food for a specialized diet)
Back scratcher target

6   Engraved, as letters on a medal
Sudden attack

7   "___ Christmas!"
Basil-based pasta sauce

8   Doing what the + sign says
Train carrier

9   Pet's main person
More-detailed section of a map

Crates

a   Percussion instrument you shake
b   Crosses home plate, in baseball
c   Making less wild
d   Get-up-and-go
e   Treat for an elephant
f   Taken without permission
g   "Not now, but soon" (3 words)
h   Little critter on a farm
i   Large, often tropical flower
j   Red flavor of Italian ice
k   Curtains
l   Grassy field
m   Bathroom fixture
n   Final meal of the day
o   Wheat, rye, oats, etc.

Hints: 184 131 87 260

LABYRINTH

Each row in this puzzle contains two answers, the second immediately following the first. The "Path" answers wind their way through the labyrinth, starting at the arrow in the upper-left corner and snaking around until finally exiting in the lower right. Clues for these answers are given in order. *Answers, page 130.*

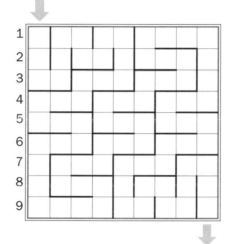

Rows

1 Word for corn that sounds like a labyrinth
Declaration of guilt or innocence, in front of a judge

2 Birds that ask "Who?"
____ out (escapes from prison)

3 Academy Award statuette
Casual word of agreement

4 Running race place
"You'd better, or ___!"

5 Neither early nor late (2 words)
What a plus sign means

6 Sunrise time, for short
Give an angry look

7 Pause in working
The way out

8 There are six of them in an inning
Flexible enough to do acrobatics

9 Home to Mount Everest
Second-to-last word of many fairy tales

Path

▶ Acts like a cow
▶ High-pitched cries
▶ Striped animal
▶ Cardboard box
▶ Musical instrument with a slide
▶ Grassy meadow
▶ A right one has 90 degrees
▶ Famed mouse of cartoons
▶ Has an entire meal (2 words)
▶ Chains on dogs
▶ It lets you reach greater heights
▶ Lumberjack's tool
▶ Alternative to spinach
▶ Hand over to somebody
▶ Metric unit of volume

Hints: 309 30 264

TRIPLE PLAY

In each puzzle below, you can move the 21 three-letter pieces into the grid to make seven 10-letter answers reading across. (You can cross out the pieces as you write them in—each will be used only once.) Clues are given for the seven words or phrases, but you'll have to figure out which clue matches each answer—they are not given in the same order. If you solve the puzzles correctly, you'll find a two-word phrase in each of them, reading down two of the columns. *Answers, page 130.*

F						
O						
P						
S						
W						
H						
A						

▶ Courtroom shouts of "My opponent can't do that!"
▶ Emergency vehicles
▶ Emergency warning that turns out not to be an emergency after all (2 words)
▶ Fifty-cent piece (2 words)
▶ Meals served between slices of bread
▶ "Tennessee" or "George Washington," grammatically (2 words)
▶ Writing surface at the front of a classroom

ALF ALS AND ARD ARM BJE CES CTI DOL EAL EBO ERN HES HIT LAN LAR MBU ONS OUN ROP WIC

G						
Q						
F						
O						
M						
S						
H						

▶ Family get-together that may involve popcorn (2 words)
▶ One of a set of five identical children
▶ Seats at the dinner table for babies
▶ Very tall building
▶ Virtue of giving to others in an unselfish way
▶ What an airplane pilot must provide before taking off (2 words)
▶ Where the president of the United States works (2 words)

CHA CRA ENE ENI GHT HTP ICE IGH IRS ITY KYS LAN LET LIG OFF OVI PER ROS TUP UIN VAL

Hints: 45 225 153 261

TWICE AROUND

Two sets of words travel clockwise around this grid. The "Once Around" answers begin at each of the numbers, 1–9. The "Twice Around" answers begin at each of the letters, a–i. Each letter is used in exactly two words. *Answers, page 130.*

Once Around

1 What you fill out when you vote
2 Red ___ (clue intended to deceive, in a mystery)
3 Mr. Lincoln, for short
4 Animal in a "red pajama," in a famous picture book
5 None at all
6 Having to do with teeth and gums
7 Bar in the shower
8 Do extremely well at
9 Successfully go on a diet (2 words)

Twice Around

a Neither this one nor that one
b Sound familiar (3 words)
c Dazzle
d Woodchuck or squirrel, for example
e In addition
f Highest point
g Large string instrument
h Use needle and thread
i It's black on a pool table (2 words)

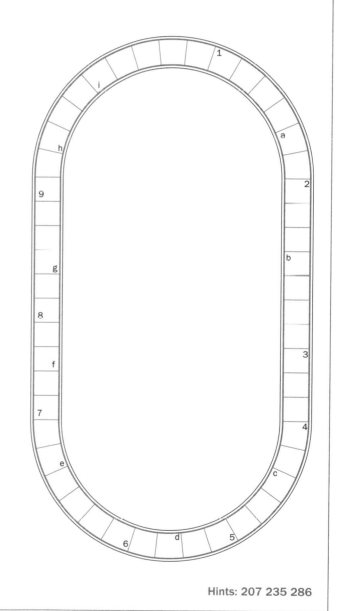

Hints: 207 235 286

TRAIL MIX

Each row contains two answers, clued in order. In addition, there are thirteen "Trails" wandering through the grid. Each trail answer begins in its numbered square and ends in one of the dotted squares—you'll have to figure out which one. Lengths of the trail answers are shown in parentheses. The thirteen trails never overlap each other, and will fill up the grid entirely. *Answers, page 131.*

A	1			2	3		●
B		●		●	4	5	
C			●		6		●
D	●	7			●		●
E						8	9
F		10	11	●	12		
G	●	●		13			●	●

Rows

A   Making something vanish, say
     Dot in the night sky

B   Cafeteria food holder
     Garden of Eden fruit

C   Yard tools used in autumn
     Place for shoes

D   Space between rooms
     An onion might cause them

E   Storage buildings, on a farm
     Sailor's "Hello there!"

F   Alternative to stairs, for wheelchair users
     Runner's place

G   Achy
     Coin toss option

Trails

1   Coast-to-coast train line (6)
2   Smoked item (5)
3   No longer edible, like bread (5)
4   ___ tense (grammar term) (4)
5   Bosc or Anjou (4)
6   Dinner with a lot of food (5)
7   Narrow space between two buildings (5)
8   Breaks into a computer (5)
9   It might have a pearl (6)
10   The Red Planet (4)
11   Fingernail coloring (6)
12   Make use of a book (4)
13   One who saves the day (4)

Hints: 73 265 47

CHECKERBOARD

Three paths of words will spiral their way into the center of this checkerboard, beginning in the upper-left corner. One path will use only the light squares. One path will use only the dark squares. And one path will use every square. You'll need to figure out where words begin and end. Word lengths for the "All Squares" answers are given. *Answers, page 131.*

All Squares

1 Seat (5)
2 Mexican money (5)
3 Red gem that is January's birthstone (6)
4 Biblical character in love with Delilah (6)
5 Expresses surprise (5)
6 Give the winner of a bet his money (3,2)
7 Not cloudy (5)
8 Onstage signals (4)
9 Sewer's need (6)
10 Eat selectively in order to lose weight (4)
11 Trial locale (5)
12 Detective's find (4)
13 Donkey's sound (4)

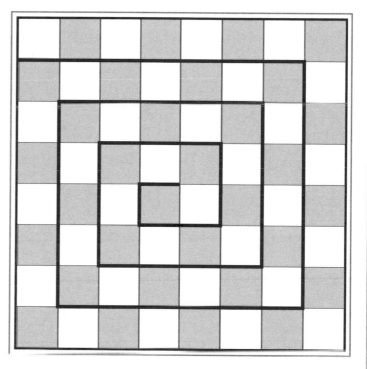

Light Squares

1 "See if I ___!"
2 Shrek, for one
3 Certain pollutants, especially in large cities
4 Pasta topping
5 Move hastily
6 Boss at a newspaper
7 Island country close to Florida

Dark Squares

1 Hula dancers shake them
2 You might visit him at the mall
3 "Make it ___!" ("Move it already!")
4 Location
5 Exchange for something else
6 Forks, knives, etc.

Hints: 247 209 298

CROSS-O

In each puzzle below, you can take the letters from one square in each column, reading left to right, to make a word. All of the words in a given puzzle belong to the same category. For example, you can make the word CIRCLE reading left to right in the first puzzle, and so now you know the category for that puzzle is SHAPES. The six categories can be seen below, but figuring out which one goes with which puzzle is up to you. *Answers, page 131.*

DISNEY MOVIES · DRINKS · INSECTS · INTERNET COMPANIES · SHAPES · US STATES

RH	QU	E	R	L̸E̸
C̸	AP	M	C̸	E
HE	I̸	A	ZO	N
S	O	AG	B	ID
TR	X	R̸	O	US

CIRCLE
_____
_____
_____
_____

LE	U	F	E	ER
W	O	LT	NA	E
J	M	T	Z	DE
C	E	I	F	EE
S	A	O	C	R

_____
_____
_____
_____
_____

DE	LI	G	ON	IA
M	R	SO	A	T
O	LA	FO	U	N
CA	RE	M	O	RE
VE	IS	W	RN	RI

_____
_____
_____
_____
_____

A	AN	Z	EL	IN
PI	ND	G	D	IO
F	N	AD	E	LA
T	RO	ER	CH	D
CI	L	OC	LE	N

_____
_____
_____
_____
_____

FI	OS	Y	I	O
L	T	E	B	LY
B	R	YD	L	UG
KA	AD	T	IT	E
M	EE	QU	F	D

_____
_____
_____
_____
_____

T	O	F	E	OK
NE	AC	C	G	T
SN	WI	O	LI	R
G	T	E	HA	LE
F	AP	TT	BO	X

_____
_____
_____
_____
_____

Hints: 270 228 157

GOTTA SPLIT

The clues in this puzzle have split! The list on the left shows the first half of every clue. The list on the right shows all of the second halves. Figure out which halves go together. When you've properly put together a clue, add up the numbers in each part. The sum matches a number in the grid, which is where the answer should be placed. *Answers, page 131.*

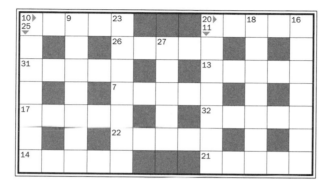

First Half

1. Doctor specializing in
2. Get-rich-quick
3. It wraps around the middle
4. Fails
5. Laughed
6. It's applied
7. Say hi
8. Cuts
9. Even more
10. Moves like
11. Speeches
12. Have the same
13. The ocean has
14. Large
15. Shape of a
16. Baby
17. Bride's
18. House made

Second Half

1. With a brush
2. Opinion
3. As you meet somebody
4. Pleasant
5. From a pulpit
6. Of the Earth
7. Frog
8. High ones and low ones
9. Walkway
10. Teeth
11. Ape
12. Into small cubes
13. Like a witch
14. Out of ice and snow
15. Game
16. Dartboard
17. A top
18. To win

Hints: 300 102 38

21

SHAPESHIFTERS

In each grid, you can make two sets of words: "Short" words by sliding the two halves together horizontally, or "Long" words by sliding the two halves together vertically. In the example shown to the right, a horizontal slide creates the short words HOP, COW, FLY, and ARM, while a vertical slide creates the longer words CHOP, FLOW, and ARMY. In each puzzle, short and long words are clued in order from top to bottom. *Answers, page 131.*

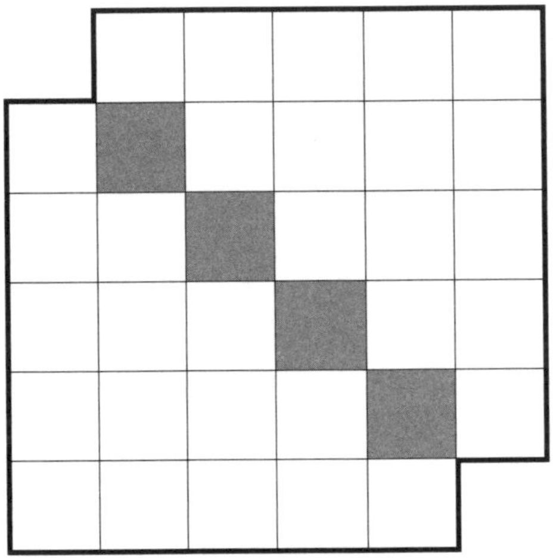

Shorts

- Express out loud
- The shark in *Finding Nemo*
- Utensil for eating soup
- Participate in a parade
- Razzle-dazzle
- One-fourth of a gallon

Longs

- One ingredient in pound cake
- ____ up (make tidy)
- Dark red color
- Momentary screw-up
- Common form of rock crystal

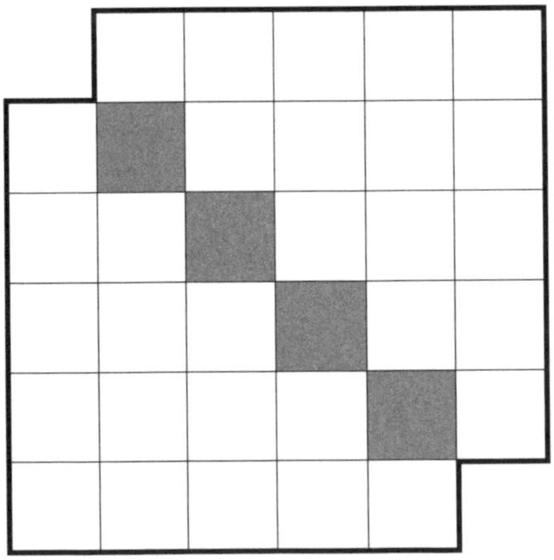

Shorts

- Go in
- Large box
- Squeeze painfully hard
- Her Royal Majesty
- Nail alternative, in a toolbox
- Small donkey used as a pack animal

Longs

- Middle
- One who attacks ships for treasure
- Satisfy, as one's thirst
- What everyone faces in a movie theater
- Underground lair (for rabbits, say)

Hints: 109 79

THREE PAIRS

In each puzzle below, fill in the blanks with the same pair of letters to make three common words. For example, if you were given S____LE, LI___T, and ____DDLE, you could fill in all three blanks with the letter pair MI, to make the words SMILE, LIMIT, and MIDDLE. The letter pairs can then be moved to the numbered blanks to spell out a familiar phrase. *Answers, page 131.*

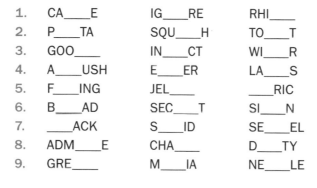

1.	CA___E	IG___RE	RHI___
2.	P___TA	SQU___H	TO___T
3.	GOO___	IN___CT	WI___R
4.	A___USH	E___ER	LA___S
5.	F___ING	JEL___	___RIC
6.	B___AD	SEC___T	SI___N
7.	___ACK	S___ID	SE___EL
8.	ADM___E	CHA___	D___TY
9.	GRE___	M___IA	NE___LE

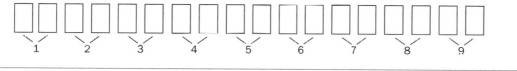

1 2 3 4 5 6 7 8 9

1.	A___ORE	SMA___	SU___I
2.	BEF___E	H___SE	MAY___
3.	S___TUE	___STY	TO___L
4.	BO___OM	MO___O	O___ER
5.	BURD___	F___CE	HY___A
6.	___GER	NA___ON	PA___O
7.	APR___	H___EST	PH___Y
8.	DI___EL	___EED	GRA___
9.	CH___GE	ORG___	P___IC

1 2 3 4 5 6 7 8 9

Hint: 236 172 115 42

ZEBRA CROSSING

Answer words go across the three rows, clued in order—you'll write one letter in each triangle. Another set of answers will go diagonally down the zebra stripes. There is one set of clues for the white stripes and another set of clues for the gray stripes, but you will need to figure out which answer goes where. *Answers, page 132.*

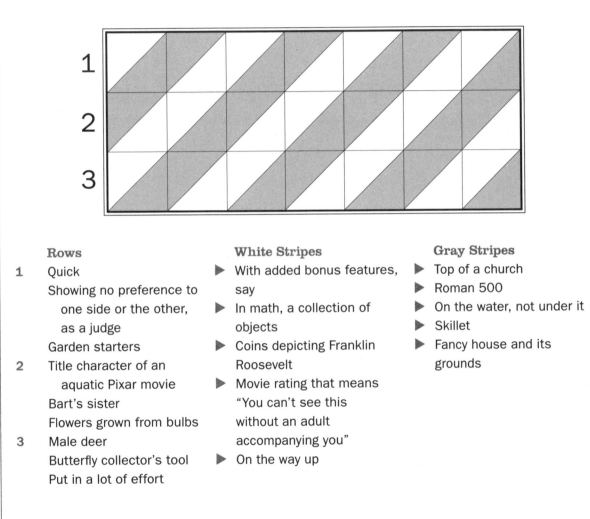

Rows

1 Quick
Showing no preference to one side or the other, as a judge
Garden starters
2 Title character of an aquatic Pixar movie
Bart's sister
Flowers grown from bulbs
3 Male deer
Butterfly collector's tool
Put in a lot of effort

White Stripes

▶ With added bonus features, say
▶ In math, a collection of objects
▶ Coins depicting Franklin Roosevelt
▶ Movie rating that means "You can't see this without an adult accompanying you"
▶ On the way up

Gray Stripes

▶ Top of a church
▶ Roman 500
▶ On the water, not under it
▶ Skillet
▶ Fancy house and its grounds

Hints: 223 322 171 190

SPIRAL

In this puzzle, one set of words will start at the 1 and spiral its way inward to the 50. Another set of words will start at the 50 and wind its way outward, back to the 1. Work back and forth between the two lists of clues until you have the whole spiral filled. *Answers, page 132.*

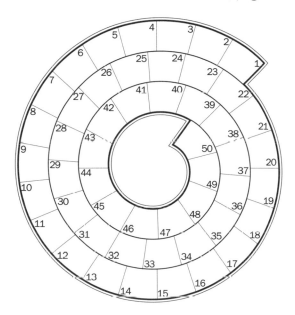

Inward

1–10: Annoys by preventing a person from succeeding

11–16: Paul who warned that "the British are coming!"

17–22: Any ship or large boat

23–29: Sang Christmas songs

30–34: *Alpha and* ____ (2010 kids' movie)

35–37: Ignited, as a match

38–42: Track meet events

43–50: Female opera singers, generally

Outward

50–46: Sensor in a submarine that detects things using "waves"

45–41: Wild West lawman's recruits to help bring in a bad guy

40–32: Flexible tissue found in your joints

31–27: Person in a fashion magazine

26–20: Ancient figures able to foretell the future

19–14: Intense, like very bad weather

13–9: Bit of poetry

8–5: Fruit-filled dessert

4–1: Ride the waves on a board

Hints: 118 304

STRIKE ONE

In each puzzle below, you can strike one letter from each word, and then push the remaining letters together to make a common word or phrase. *Answers, page 132.*

Example:
ǾROLL ER/C ŢOASTER   <u>ROLLERCOASTER</u>

1. CANDY LEAST PICK   _____

2. EAT GLENS COURT   _____

3. PAYS TARSAL AID   _____

4. BARB YES BITTER   _____

5. COAX THANK GEAR   _____

6. FAIL SETTEE THE   _____

7. SCAR KAPPA PEAR   _____

8. BASTE BALLET EXAM   _____

9. ACRE DITCH ARID   _____

10. ECRU ISLES CHIP   _____

11. WEED DINGED RESTS   _____

12. TORCHES TRAMP KIT   _____

13. LICHEN STEP LATTE   _____

14. MEG TENORS HOWLER   _____

Hints: 12 161 217

ONE TWO THREE

This is a regular crossword puzzle except for one small thing: Each box will receive one, two, or three letters. The answer to 1-Across has been written in, as an example and to get you started. *Answers, page 132.*

¹B	²AS	³SES		⁴	⁵	⁶
⁷				⁸		
	⁹	¹⁰		¹¹		
		¹²	¹³			
		¹⁴				
	¹⁵			¹⁶	¹⁷	
¹⁸	¹⁹			²⁰	²¹	²²
²³				²⁴		

Across

1 Guitars that play low notes
4 Frodo's race, in *Lord of the Rings*
7 Neighbor of Ohio
8 Absolutely destroys
9 Parking-spot coin collector
11 Lumber material
12 The Nile, for example
14 Loses a staring contest
15 Edible ice cream holder
16 What an optimist has
18 Lack of noise
20 After-the-storm sight
23 Car you buy only temporarily
24 Had a feeling

Down

1 Tie together
2 Like someone from China or Korea
3 ____ Street
4 Souped-up car (2 words)
5 Great big party
6 Uses one's teeth on
10 Awful
11 Studio for a woodworker or other craftsperson
13 Blood carrier
15 Keep out of sight
17 Remove pencil marks
18 Ambulance's noisemaker
19 Period before Easter
21 Small, cozy hotels
22 Received applause graciously

Hints: 117 64 283

WORD SQUARES

In each puzzle below, the five answers to the clues can be placed into the grid so that they form a word square—that is, each word will read both across and down, as in the example to the right. The clues are not given in order—you'll have to figure out which word goes where. *Answers, page 132.*

H	E	A	R	T
E	M	B	E	R
A	B	U	S	E
R	E	S	I	N
T	R	E	N	D

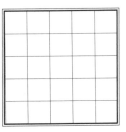

▶ Acted depressed
▶ Game where you balance wooden blocks
▶ Mental flashes
▶ State your point of view
▶ Symbol used in text messages

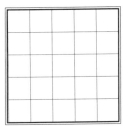

▶ Blood carriers, in the body
▶ Small black or green fruit used in oils
▶ New Delhi is its capital
▶ One who prefers to keep to himself
▶ Delete

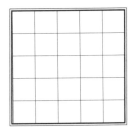

▶ Homes for robins
▶ Set of eight
▶ Presents
▶ She went to Wonderland
▶ Wheeled toy that's often red

▶ Audibly
▶ Military action figure from Hasbro (2 words)
▶ One who doesn't eat meat, milk, or eggs
▶ Person banned from a country
▶ Requires

Hints: 308 275 49 3

TO AND FRO

Exactly half of the twenty-four words in this crossword will be entered normally . . . but the other half will be entered backward—which is to say, from right to left for Across entries, or from the bottom to the top for Down entries. *Answers, page 132.*

Across

1 Places to sleep
4 In pain
7 Part of Congress with 100 members
8 Eastern, Central, Mountain, or Pacific, in the United States (2 words)
9 *Frozen*'s snowman
11 Mammal at an aquarium (2 words)
13 Popular concert acts are asked for a lot of them
17 More than just a few pimples
19 "I hope you do well!" (2 words)
20 Like something that can't be believed
21 Richly green, as a beautiful lawn
22 Little cut, with scissors

Down

1 They're twirled by majorettes
2 Tart green fruit
3 Had crazy visions while sleeping
4 Brownish-greenish eye color
5 Information on a dog collar
6 To the left, on a map
10 America's 16th president
12 Bird commonly found in large cities
14 Dad's brother
15 Word of greeting
16 Anakin's son, in *Star Wars*
18 De-wrinkling device

Hints: 74 194 124 56

HEXED

Each six-letter answer in this puzzle will be entered around its number, starting in the space with the arrow and proceeding in the direction the arrow points (like SAMPLE in the example to the right). As extra assistance, the top row of hexes and the bottom row of hexes will have the same letters in the same order. *Answers, page 133.*

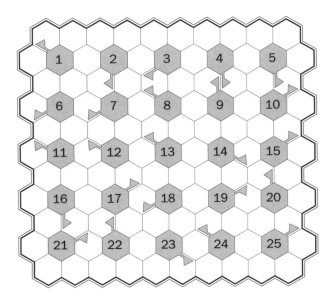

1 1, 2, or 3, for example	15 Color of a penny
2 Quantity	16 Homes away from home
3 Fabric found in many shirts	17 Less well tied, as a knot
4 Gets on, as a horse	18 Nurtures from a baby to an adult
5 Rarely	19 Clears the whiteboard
6 Small rock	20 The world has over seven billion of them
7 Took a turn facing the pitcher	21 Say "No videogames for a week!," for example
8 Partner in running the show	22 Husband or wife
9 "Hello" in Hebrew	23 Threw (a ball)
10 Big, wet kiss	24 Nearby
11 Whistler on the stovetop	25 Curly haired dog breed
12 Rang (a bell)	
13 Outgoing; with many friends	
14 Locations	

Hints: 93 206 147

ROWS GARDEN

One or two words can be placed in each row of this small "garden." The answer to each "Bloom" clue, all of which are six letters long, should be put into the appropriately numbered flower, but it's up to you to figure out the starting petal and whether the answer reads clockwise or counterclockwise. *Answers, page 133.*

Rows

A Just purchased and still unused

B Bother
   Gets ready to shoot

C Make beer or coffee or a magic potion
   Bowler's place

D Defense of a particular *Ghostbusters* ghost
   Not any

E Newborn cow
   At the start of a line

F Number of judges on the Supreme Court
   Open the door for (2 words)

G Stare at in wonder
   Trims back

H Stopover point for travelers

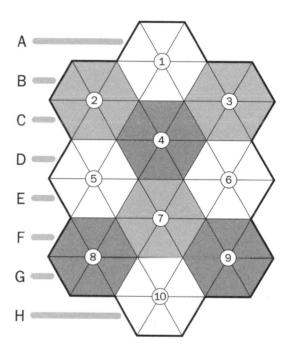

Blooms

1 Traffic-directing sign (2 words)
2 Large flag
3 ☺
4 Sheriffs and the like
5 Purple flowers
6 Some male vocalists
7 Gustave ____, designer of a famous tower in Paris
8 Shade over a storefront
9 "____ Coin" (arcade game words)
10 Paper or cloth item next to a dinner plate

Hints: 107 2 325

FOR STARTERS

It's not often that you can solve two puzzles at the same time, but that's what you'll be doing here. The clues to the two grids are all mixed together. The answers are all five-letter words, and each begins with a different letter of the alphabet. Those starting letters have already been placed for you. Can you use the given letters and the clues provided to complete both grids? *Answers, page 133.*

	F	I	Y	G
O				
Q				
S				
W				

	A	R	C	H
B				
M				
K				
L				

▶ Black bird
▶ By yourself
▶ DNA stuff
▶ Film
▶ Gives away, but expects back
▶ High ____ (kind of shoes)
▶ Instrument related to the piccolo
▶ Joins together with a searing hot flame, as two pieces of metal
▶ King's wife
▶ Make a loud, harsh noise
▶ Past its sell-by date, perhaps
▶ Perfect
▶ Road sign that means "Let the other cars go first"
▶ Song that was popular many decades ago, say
▶ Wept
▶ What some people do before praying

Hints: 310 48 132

FLOWER POWER

Twelve answers in this flower-shaped grid will be entered clockwise, beginning from each numbered space and curving inward to the center. The other twelve answers will be entered counterclockwise, beginning from those same spaces. Work back and forth until you have completed the grid. *Answers, page 133.*

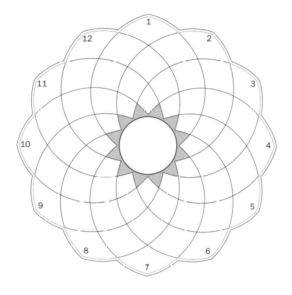

Clockwise

1. Said in a nonserious way
2. Friend on the pirate ship
3. Farm buildings
4. Bert's buddy
5. View from the International Space Station
6. More than merely bad
7. Bamboo-loving "bear"
8. Some bait
9. Office notes
10. Not a soul (2 words)
11. Item near most desks
12. Number of "deadly sins"

Counterclockwise

1. Casual pants
2. Theatrical showing
3. One who makes a lot of dough?
4. No longer on the plate
5. Made a mistake
6. Child-care assistant
7. Eiffel Tower locale
8. Not use wisely, as resources
9. One-twelfth of the year
10. Uncool
11. Midsentence punctuation mark
12. Chases (away)

Hints: 250 324 214

BIRDS OF A FEATHER

The 22 birds listed below can be placed into the grid, one bird per row, always reading across. Letters in the larger areas will be shared by more than one bird, as demonstrated at right, where SAMPLE and EXAMPLE share their final five letters. Can you get the entire flock together? *Answers, page 133.*

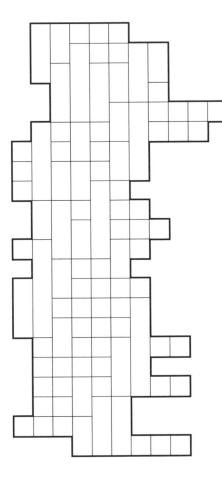

ALBATROSS · CANARY · CARDINAL · CONDOR · EAGLE · FALCON · FLAMINGO ·
HERON · KESTREL · OSPREY · OSTRICH · PARROT · PARTRIDGE · PEACOCK · PELICAN ·
PENGUIN · PUFFIN · SPARROW · SWALLOW · SWIFT · TANAGER · WARBLER

Hints: 227 293

TWO BY TWO

In each puzzle, you can place the nine pairs of letters into the grid to make nine words—four reading across and five reading down. Pieces should not be rotated or flipped. Clues are given for the nine words in each puzzle, but you'll have to figure out where each answer should be placed. *Answers, page 134.*

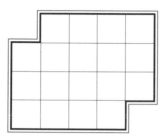

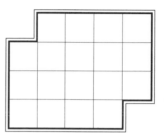

- Beaver's structure
- Each one in a pair
- ____ hall (where soldiers eat)
- See eye to eye
- Part of the body that includes the cornea and the retina
- Place where they bottle milk, make cheese, etc.
- Puts on television or on the radio
- Spanish for "three"
- Wizard

- Apple tablet
- "Approximately" (2 words)
- Body of water smaller than a lake
- Empty space
- Flavor of purple candy, generally
- Leave out
- Like someone from the largest continent
- Start of many a countdown
- ____ Street (common name in many American towns)

Hints: 92 289

YOU CAN QUOTE ME

Write the answer to each clue on the dashes, and then transfer each letter to its correspondingly numbered square in the grid to spell out a quotation from Albert Einstein. Words in the quote that don't end on one line will continue on the next. Black squares separate the words of the quote. As you fill in letters in the quote, try to figure out some of its words—doing so will in turn help you with the answers to the clues. An extra bit of assistance: The dozen answers below are in alphabetical order. *Answers, page 134.*

1C		2H	3E	4G	5A	6K		7A	8L	9B		10L	11J	12G	13C	14K
15D	16L	17F		18B	19G	20C	21L	22J	23K		24H	25I	26B		27E	28C	29B
30J	31L	•		32F	33K	34A	35D	36H	37J	—	38G	39C	40K	41E		42G	43L
44I	45A	46C		47H	48D	49L		50A	51F	52K	53L	54C	55G	56H	57I	58B	59L
	60K	61G		62C	63K	64E	65D	66H	•		67K	68C	69I		70F	71L	72B
73D	74K	75A	76G	77J	78E		79E	80B	81J	82G		83D		84E	85H		86L
87C	88K	89H	90A	•												

A. Hiker's water-holder
___ ___ ___ ___ ___ ___ ___
50 7 34 90 45 75 5

B. Mineral that is the hardest naturally occurring substance on Earth
___ ___ ___ ___ ___ ___ ___
26 80 29 18 58 72 9

C. Where a running race ends (2 words)
___ ___ ___ ___ ___ ___ ___ ___ ___ ___
62 1 13 39 46 68 54 87 20 28

D. Used a rod and reel
___ ___ ___ ___ ___ ___
15 83 65 48 35 73

E. Free of any illness
___ ___ ___ ___ ___ ___ ___
78 41 84 64 79 3 27

F. Trumpet or bugle
___ ___ ___ ___
70 51 17 32

G. 2016 Oscar winner for Best Animated Feature Film (2 words)
___ ___ ___ ___ ___ ___ ___ ___ ___
12 38 61 4 76 82 19 55 42

H. Exam covering fractions, exponents, etc. (2 words)
___ ___ ___ ___ ___ ___ ___ ___
85 24 47 89 36 66 56 2

I. Word shouted by a possessive toddler
___ ___ ___ ___
44 57 25 69

J. The "beat" of music
___ ___ ___ ___ ___ ___
30 11 37 77 22 81

K. Place to glide on the ice (2 words)
___ ___ ___ ___ ___ ___ ___ ___ ___ ___ ___
23 14 63 67 33 52 88 74 60 40 6

L. One of many at Wimbledon (2 words)
___ ___ ___ ___ ___ ___ ___ ___ ___ ___ ___
10 49 59 8 43 31 53 16 71 86 21

Hints: 251 156 306

LABYRINTH

Each row in this puzzle contains two answers, the second immediately following the first. The "Path" answers wind their way through the labyrinth, starting at the arrow in the upper-left corner and snaking around until finally exiting in the lower right. Clues for these answers are given in order. *Answers, page 134.*

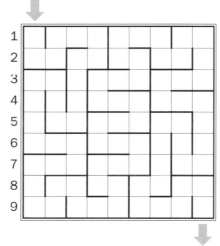

Rows

1 Exchange for money
   Grasps with one's hands
2 Uppermost room in some
      houses
   Tidy
3 Song meant for two
   Nickname for Dad,
      sometimes
4 Walk leisurely
   Google competitor from
      Microsoft
5 Small, short-winged
      songbird
   Round numbers?
6 Knight's protective wear
   Top of the line

7 Color associated with envy
   Sticky stuff that comes
      in a roll
8 Started over, as a project
   Get somebody angry
9 Mexican building material
   Hired housecleaner

Path

▶ Object in orbit around the
   Earth
▶ Island nation near the East
   Coast of the United States
▶ "Getting closer!" in a
   children's game
▶ Marked a test paper
▶ Like a well-trained dog

▶ Metal in the third-place
   medal
▶ It's useful when your pants
   are baggy
▶ Sleeveless, waterproof
   outerwear with a hood
▶ Starring roles
▶ Using a device to listen in
   on phone calls
▶ One foot forward
▶ Slightly hurt
▶ Sent a package overseas

Hints: 249 90 291

TRAIL MIX

Each row contains two answers, clued in order. In addition, there are twelve "Trails" wandering through the grid. Each trail answer begins in its numbered square and ends in one of the dotted squares—you'll have to figure out which one. Lengths of the trail answers are shown in parentheses. The twelve trails never overlap each other, and will fill up the grid entirely. *Answers, page 134.*

Rows

A Move to the rhythm
   Composer Johann Sebastian
B Like some fails, in slang
   "Home on the ____"
C Sour-tasting fruit
   Trick-or-treater's purchase
D Item of footwear
   One of Columbus's ships
E French word for "love"
   TV show with lots of musical numbers,
      2009–2015
F Chip at a Mexican restaurant
   Exterminator's target
G Understands
   Prepares a potato, perhaps

Trails

1 Singer with the 2015 hit "Hello" (5)
2 Loud noises (5)
3 Soreness (4)
4 Crab's claw (6)
5 He'll cheat you out of your money (3,3)
6 Ask for something without paying for it (5)
7 France's continent (6)
8 Little oinker (6)
9 T-bone, for one (5)
10 Grind together, as your teeth when you're
   angry (5)
11 You'll find it over a boiling pot (5)
12 Snooze (5)

Hints: 299 91 44

40   Eric Berlin

PACKING CRATES

Two words will go in each row of this grid, clued in order. Another set of words can be found in the fifteen "Crates," always reading row by row, as demonstrated in the examples to the right. Can you pack the crates with all the right answers? *Answers, page 134.*

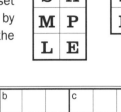

Rows

1 Show live on the Internet
  Word processor command when you've made a mistake
2 Amusement park feature
  Wealth
3 Las ____, Nevada
  Put a seed in the ground
4 Electrical cable
  Cookbook instructions
5 Sporting-event venue
  Former New York Yankee Jeter
6 Prefix that means "half"
  Made a dramatic basket, in basketball
7 Seat
  List at the end of a book
8 Mouse or squirrel
  A single time
9 Gold is a precious one
  Window ledges

Crates

a Try hard to reach a goal
b Book lover
c Large city in Germany
d Contraction meaning "fails to"
e Place where vegetables grow
f Put peanut butter on bread
g More delicate and frilly
h Rough, as sandpaper
i Closed your eyes, but not really
j Where trapeze artists meet
k Not nice
l Google's Internet browser
m Does great (at)
n Regarding the teeth
o Oft-removed body part, found in the throat

Hints: 199 313 231 331

RIDING THE WAVES

Answers follow two paths in this grid—two answers will go into each row, and two answers will go into each of the zigzagging "Waves." You'll have to determine where one answer ends and the next one begins. When the grid is complete, the gray spaces at the very top and bottom of the grid will spell out a famous wave-riding vessel. *Answers, page 134.*

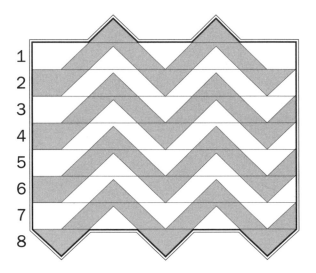

Rows

1 Dismiss from a job
   What this answer won't be if you get it
      right
2 Area in a house
   Shaver's needs
3 Two squared
   Tiny insects that feed on plants
4 Prom-goer's purchase
   Reprimand for a wrongdoing
5 Dream up
   Payments
6 Where the bride and groom stand as they
      get married
   Cowboy's ride
7 Femur or tibia
   Neatened one's hair, maybe

Waves

2 Ready to eat, as a banana
   Pickle juice
3 Like tuxedos and gowns
   Chances (that a certain thing will happen)
4 Ways in or out
   Beach toys that accompany shovels
5 Some sandwich makers cut them off
   Prepared the ground for planting
6 In math, length times width
   Break from school
7 Whitening additive, for laundry
   Not costing anything
8 Dot on a musical staff
   "So sorry to hear it" (2 words)

Hints: 208 70

CHECKERBOARD

Three paths of words will spiral their way into the center of this checkerboard, beginning in the upper-left corner. One path will use only the light squares. One path will use only the dark squares. And one path will use every square. You'll need to figure out where words begin and end. Word lengths for the "All Squares" answers are given. *Answers, page 135.*

All Squares

1 SpongeBob SquarePants has a pet one (5)
2 Sewing kit item (6)
3 "It's a Hard-Knock Life" musical (5)
4 Some writing assignments from school (6)
5 Frequent skin problem among teenagers (4)
6 You fasten your shoelaces with one (4)
7 Look (through, as a telescope) (4)
8 Piece of pasta (6)
9 Like water you can't stand in (4)
10 Funny television show (6)
11 Only mammals that fly (4)
12 From China, for example (5)
13 Unwanted plants in the garden (5)

Light Squares

1 Store event with lower prices
2 Refuses to accept
3 Hard pull
4 Ready for business for the day
5 Like the first-born child, compared to any siblings
6 Got ahold of, as a needed item

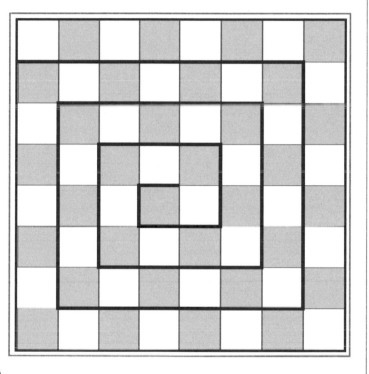

Dark Squares

1 Number of people on a baseball team
2 Many highways have three of them
3 Trip to the top of a mountain
4 Wear away naturally
5 Like a story that takes four hours to tell
6 Church service
7 Astounds

Hints: 205 314 245

AROUND THE BEND

Each answer in this puzzle starts in the appropriately numbered square . . . but when you run out of room in that row, you'll follow the arrow and write the rest of the answer backward in the next row down. This will then be the start of the next answer on the list. For example, the last three letters of PLAID in the small grid to the right become the first three letters of the next answer, DIARY. The grid below forms a loop—the first and last rows will be the same. *Answers, page 135.*

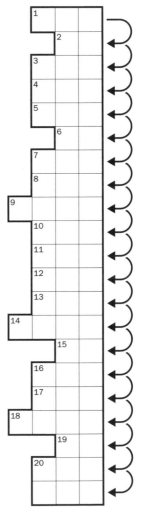

1 Spanish "mister"
2 Large houses have a lot of them
3 Campfire treats
4 Brought food out to the diners, at a restaurant
5 Halloween costume with a pitchfork
6 Light-purple flower
7 Person on the phone
8 On the same family tree
9 Small points of a large plan
10 Tricky baseball pitch
11 Feature on most phones
12 Sick or injured and stuck in bed (2 words)
13 Small pools after a storm
14 Not often
15 Was visibly depressed
16 Leave
17 Preview of a movie
18 Archaeologists collect them
19 Patch of skin under your hair
20 Airborne vessels

Hints: 211 53

BITS AND PIECES

The first column of clues will lead to a series of three- or four-letter answers. (Three-letter answers go in the gray boxes and four-letter answers in the white boxes.) You can use the letters in any two neighboring boxes—along with an additional letter, which you must determine—to spell the eight-letter word clued on the right. For example, if your three-letter word was SIP, and your four-letter word was RUST, you could mix them with an additional A to make the word UPSTAIRS. The letters you add will spell an appropriate phrase, reading down. *Answers, page 135.*

| SIP | A | UPSTAIRS |
| RUST | | |

Clues (left)			Clues (right)
Fruity drink, often lemon-flavored			Explosive stuff
Toothpaste flavor			Like movies where people fall in love
Automobile			Nabs, like a wanted criminal
Animals in the home			Main ingredient in french fries
Also			Window in a ship
Give assistance to			Toy you play with by blowing on it
Come in first			Colorful sights after the storm
Steals (from)			Shellfish with large claws
Six games of tennis wins it			Make a mess, with paint
Device for catching a mouse			Crushed underfoot
Was ahead in points, in a game			Some defensive players, in baseball
Football officials			A doctor tests these by hitting you with a hammer
Long, snakelike fish			More tired
Tears a hole in			Ran in a track meet, perhaps
X, in Roman numerals			XIV, in Roman numerals
"Watch out for that golf ball!"			Playground game where you jump over people
Period of slowness, on the Net			

Hints: 31 1

GOTTA SPLIT

The clues in this puzzle have split! The list on the left shows the first half of every clue. The list on the right shows all of the second halves. Figure out which halves go together. When you've properly put together a clue, add up the numbers in each part. The sum matches a number in the grid, which is where the answer should be placed. *Answers, page 135.*

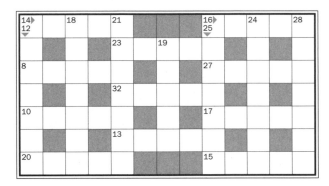

	First Half		Second Half
1	Difficult to	1	A little bit shy
2	Main ingredient	2	Lost
3	Where you'll see	3	Let you leave
4	Prefix that can start	4	At the zoo
5	Hit that goes	5	For many travelers
6	Get	6	Rock
7	Holes	7	In a trash can
8	Language spoken	8	In cakes and bread
9	Parent's	9	"Line" or "ground"
10	No longer	10	Offspring
11	Dwarf who is	11	Lots of sand
12	Like animals	12	In Ancient Rome
13	Arrival point	13	Fancy clothes (2 words)
14	Doors that	14	Climb, like a hill
15	Put on	15	Out of one's home
16	*Sesame Street* resident	16	Over the wall (2 words)
17	Kick	17	Sleeping
18	Very hard	18	In the moon

Hints: 189 263 55

CROSSFIRE

First, answer as many clues as you can. Each answer on the left side can be matched up to an answer on the right, via a rule that you'll have to determine. Word lengths for all answers are given. When you've paired up two words, carefully draw a straight line connecting the dot of one clue to the dot of the other. You will cross off some of the letters. After you've matched up all the words, the remaining letters, reading down, will spell an appropriate movie title. *Answers, page 136.*

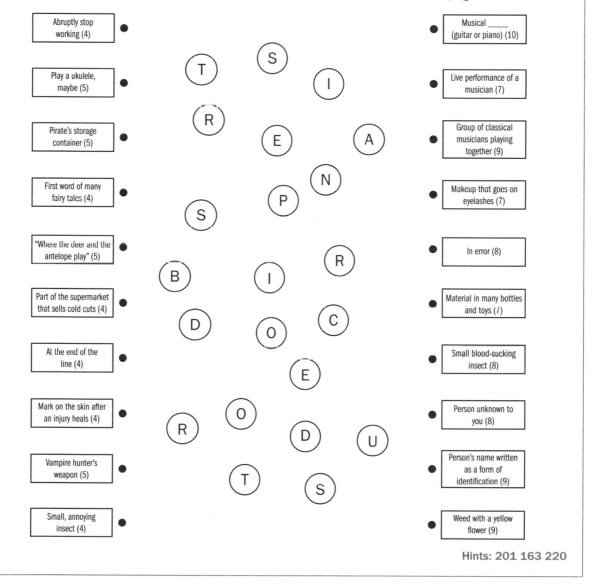

Abruptly stop working (4)

Play a ukulele, maybe (5)

Pirate's storage container (5)

First word of many fairy tales (4)

"Where the deer and the antelope play" (5)

Part of the supermarket that sells cold cuts (4)

At the end of the line (4)

Mark on the skin after an injury heals (4)

Vampire hunter's weapon (5)

Small, annoying insect (4)

Musical _____ (guitar or piano) (10)

Live performance of a musician (7)

Group of classical musicians playing together (9)

Makeup that goes on eyelashes (7)

In error (8)

Material in many bottles and toys (7)

Small blood-sucking insect (8)

Person unknown to you (8)

Person's name written as a form of identification (9)

Weed with a yellow flower (9)

Hints: 201 163 220

CROSS-O

In each puzzle below, you can take the letters from one square in each column, reading left to right, to make a word or phrase. All of the words in a given puzzle belong to the same category. For example, you can make the word DIAMOND reading left to right in the first puzzle, and so now you know the category for that puzzle is GEMSTONES. The six categories can be seen below, but figuring out which one goes with which puzzle is up to you. *Answers, page 136.*

BREAKFAST FOODS · GEMSTONES · HALLOWEEN COSTUMES · REPTILES · STYLES OF MUSIC · THINGS IN A BATHROOM

E	P	R	~~ON~~	RE
T	~~A~~	N	OI	LD
GA	UR	~~M~~	A	T
~~DI~~	R	PH	E	SE
SA	ME	QU	I	~~D~~

DIAMOND

L	GU	R	K	LE
G	O	A	R	E
CR	U	ZA	N	O
I	E	CO	TL	D
T	I	C	DI	A

WE	AM	M	OL	H
Z	E	T	IR	N
V	I	LE	B	F
W	O	EW	TO	E
SK	R	P	C	IE

B	P	SI	ET	RY
CL	AV	U	T	AL
HI	L	UN	O	S
C	AS	YM	E	L
HE	O	H	CA	P

SH	O	HP	DI	O
PL	OA	M	AS	ER
T	A	N	E	SH
S	OT	P	G	TE
TO	U	W	PO	L

O	A	E	U	T
CE	O	CA	O	E
PA	ME	C	A	RT
Y	R	L	E	N
B	N	G	K	L

Hints: 285 66 239

20 QUESTIONS

Cross out each of the words identified by the twenty clues shown below. When you're done, you'll have five words left in the circle. These can be arranged to spell out a quote by John Wooden. *Answers, page 136.*

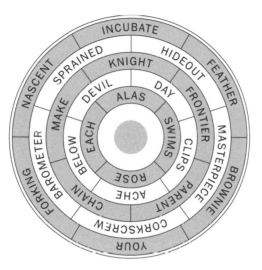

Which word . . .

1. . . . becomes a country when you move the third letter to the end?
2. . . . becomes a new word if you remove the first letter, the first two letters, or the first three letters?
3. . . . sounds like a phrase meaning "belonging to royalty"?
4. . . . becomes a new word when you place an E on each end?
5. . . . is a part of the body when you read only the odd-numbered letters?
6. . . . becomes a new word when spelled backward?
7. . . . becomes a country when you remove the first and last pair of letters?
8. . . . contains a world capital?
9. . . . can be read in a silly way to mean "closer to the start of the line"?
10. . . . contains five consonants in a row?
11. . . . is a form of weather inside a word meaning "went fast"?
12. . . . becomes a girl's name when you place an R at the start and an L at the end?
13. . . . is a family member when you drop the second letter?
14. . . . contains only the letters found in PETER PAN?
15. . . . reads the same when turned upside down?
16. . . . contains three silent letters?
17. . . . can be either a noun or a past-tense verb?
18. . . . is the start of one of the United States?
19. . . . becomes a word meaning "yell" when you double one of its letters?
20. . . . becomes a word meaning "horrible" when you move the last letter back one in the alphabet (so B ➜ A or C ➜ B, etc.)?

Hints: 256 104 25

PINWHEEL

Each ring of the pinwheel will contain two or more answers, starting at the numbered space and reading clockwise. Another set of words will begin in the space indicated by the arrow, and proceed to the right, in a path that winds up and down around the grid. Lengths are given for all answers. *Answers, page 136.*

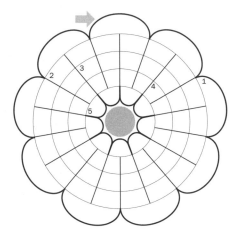

Rings

1 Feel concern (about) (4)
   One of two choices on certain tests (5)
2 Like the end of the pool where the diving
     board is (7)
   Deodorant's target (6)
   Toys that are only good in windy
     weather (5)
3 Woman's alternative to pants (5)
   Your parent's brothers (6)
   Breathed in (7)
4 Sport where you might wield a lasso (5)
   Bottoms of your shoes (5)
   Flying an aircraft (8)
5 Flip-down part of an airplane seat (4)
   One who prefers his own company (5)

Path

▶ Turn, like a pinwheel (4)
▶ Has the same opinion (6)
▶ Audition (6)
▶ Good thing to have during a blackout (6)
▶ Study fast and hard for a test (4)
▶ Like a sloppily tied knot (5)
▶ "The big house," to criminals (6)
▶ Word on a low-calorie food's packaging (4)
▶ Mid-leg joint (4)
▶ Keyboard key that gives you capital
   letters (5)
▶ Springtime month (5)
▶ Painter's stand (5)
▶ Walk like a three-year-old (6)
▶ Umpire's call (6)

Hints: 252 168 77

CROSS ANAGRAMS

In each puzzle below, clues are given in pairs. Write the answer to the first clue in each pair in the left-side grid, and the second answer in the right-side grid. The two answers will be anagrams of each other—that is, they use the same letters but in a different order. When each grid is complete, a phrase will be seen running diagonally down the gray squares of the two grids. *Answers, page 137.*

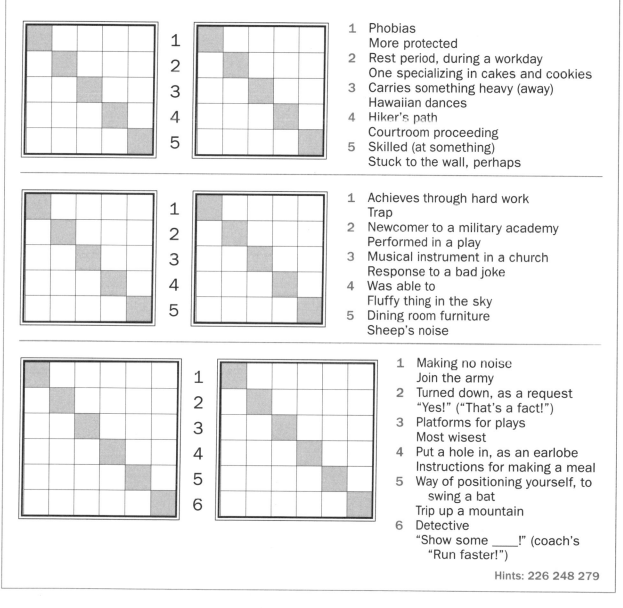

1 Phobias
  More protected
2 Rest period, during a workday
  One specializing in cakes and cookies
3 Carries something heavy (away)
  Hawaiian dances
4 Hiker's path
  Courtroom proceeding
5 Skilled (at something)
  Stuck to the wall, perhaps

1 Achieves through hard work
  Trap
2 Newcomer to a military academy
  Performed in a play
3 Musical instrument in a church
  Response to a bad joke
4 Was able to
  Fluffy thing in the sky
5 Dining room furniture
  Sheep's noise

1 Making no noise
  Join the army
2 Turned down, as a request
  "Yes!" ("That's a fact!")
3 Platforms for plays
  Most wisest
4 Put a hole in, as an earlobe
  Instructions for making a meal
5 Way of positioning yourself, to
    swing a bat
  Trip up a mountain
6 Detective
  "Show some ____!" (coach's
    "Run faster!")

Hints: 226 248 279

FLOWER POWER

Twelve answers in this flower-shaped grid will be entered clockwise, beginning from each numbered space and curving inward to the center. The other twelve answers will be entered counterclockwise, beginning from those same spaces. Work back and forth until you have completed the grid. *Answers, page 137.*

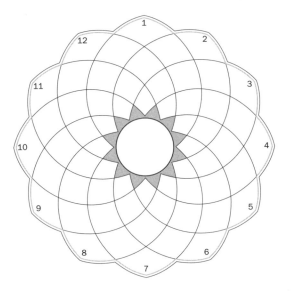

Clockwise

1. Small bush
2. Trapped behind bars
3. One of your teeth
4. Under
5. Animal in a desert caravan
6. Grouchy and rude
7. Horned African animal
8. Upper leg
9. Come down with, as a cold
10. Put to work again
11. Miserable
12. Blackens on the stovetop

Counterclockwise

1. "Quiet!"
2. Exciting part of some movies
3. Walk down the aisle together
4. Phony
5. Movie star or other famous person, in brief
6. Leafy precursor to the main course
7. Story getting passed around
8. Pitched (a ball)
9. "Relax!"
10. Requiring an umbrella
11. "Unhand me!" (2 words)
12. Furniture item in the living room

Hints: 159 303 105

ONE TWO THREE

This is a regular crossword puzzle except for one small thing: Each box will receive one, two, or three letters. The answer to 1-Across has been written in, as an example and to get you started. *Answers, page 137.*

¹S	²PI	³GOT				⁴	⁵	⁶
⁷						⁸		
		⁹	¹⁰		¹¹			
			¹²	¹³				
			¹⁴					
		¹⁵			¹⁶	¹⁷		
¹⁸	¹⁹					²⁰	²¹	²²
²³						²⁴		

Across

1   Faucet
4   Dueling weapon
7   Fasten together
8   Sport for cowboys
9   Lemon- or lime-flavored drink
11 Perform on the ice
12 Thick wire
14 Feature of many babies' smiles
15 Untruths
16 Where your taste buds are
18 Harry's friend, at Hogwarts
20 Earn points
23 Say a prayer over
24 Silvery stuff for the Christmas tree

Down

1   Used a chair
2   Bread with a pocket
3   "Aha! Caught you!"
4   Blackbeard, for one
5   Got up from a chair
6   Zodiac sign preceding Virgo
10 Groups of ten years
11 You have one inside you
13 Floating airship
15 Female head of a pride
17 "Be Our ____" (Disney song)
18 Parsley, sage, rosemary, or thyme
19 1,760 yards
21 Loose change, generally
22 Part of a fishing rod

Hints: 148 84 103

HEXED

Each six-letter answer in this puzzle will be entered around its number, starting in the space with the arrow and proceeding in the direction the arrow points (like SAMPLE in the example to the right). As extra assistance, the top row of hexes and the bottom row of hexes will have the same letters in the same order. *Answers, page 137.*

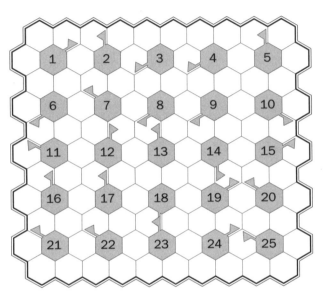

1. The capital of Colorado
2. Directions that must be followed
3. Dried grape
4. Crossed home plate, say
5. Express embarrassment, perhaps
6. Part of a shirt
7. Unit of measurement for temperature
8. Making an attempt
9. Solution to a problem
10. Say "Remember your mom's birthday next week!"
11. Puts in the fridge for a while
12. Small disturbance on the surface of a pond
13. Heart, in slang
14. Music player, often with two speakers
15. Harry of children's literature
16. State you can't drive to
17. Say something after being quiet (2 words)
18. Front of a belt
19. Items that are neither liquid nor gaseous
20. Subjects (of conversation)
21. Roam aimlessly
22. Individual
23. Fry and then stew in a little liquid
24. Some dance clubs
25. Like the view from the Grand Canyon

Hints: 179 295 6

YOU CAN QUOTE ME

Write the answer to each clue on the dashes, and then transfer each letter to its correspondingly numbered square in the grid to spell out a quotation from A. A. Milne. Words in the quote that don't end on one line will continue on the next. Black squares separate the words of the quote. As you fill in letters in the quote, try to figure out some of its words—doing so will in turn help you with the answers to the clues. An extra bit of assistance: The dozen answers below are in alphabetical order. *Answers, page 137.*

1L	2A	3D		4D	5E		6J	7G	8H		9D	10C	11D	12C	13I	14F
15J	16I	17G	18L		19C	20F		21A	22B	23F	24K	25J		26C	27A	28G
29I	30D	31G	32K	33J	34D	35L		36G	37H		38L	39J	40B	41K		42F
43B	44D		45J	46G		47E	48C	49I	50K	51L	52B	53F	54H	55J	56L
57B	58C	59A	60K	61J	62I		63E	64K	65B	66A	67D	68F	69H	70J		71C
72I	73E	74F	75L	76D	77K	78L	79A	80J	81H	•						

A. Two-piece bathing suit
__ __ __ __ __ __
21 27 59 66 2 79

B. Stone Age fellow
__ __ __ __ __ __ __
65 40 11 22 57 52 43

C. Thingamabob; gizmo
__ __ __ __ __ __
10 48 19 26 58 71

D. Skyscraper's vertical transport
__ __ __ __ __ __ __ __
3 34 44 76 9 67 4 30

E. Stands looking toward
__ __ __ __ __
5 12 47 63 73

F. Made-up stories
__ __ __ __ __ __ __
20 23 74 14 68 42 53

G. Made a sound like a snake
__ __ __ __ __ __
7 36 28 46 17 31

H. Birds' homes
__ __ __ __ __
69 8 37 54 81

I. Slang for the head
__ __ __ __ __ __
13 29 16 62 72 49

J. In geometry, it has 90 degrees (2 words)
__ __ __ __ __ __ __ __ __ __
33 45 25 39 6 15 61 70 55 80

K. Sweet ____ (big birthday party, for) some
__ __ __ __ __ __ __
50 60 64 41 32 77 24

L. Pixar's first feature film (2 words)
__ __ __ __ __ __ __ __
51 75 35 18 38 1 78 56

Hints: 290 182 86

HALF AND HALF

In this puzzle, you'll spell a series of six-letter words, with half the letters in one box and half in another. Each pair of boxes connected by a line will spell the word clued by that line's number. All words read from left to right. The first and last boxes in the chain will contain the same letters, as with MANTLE, BATTLE, and BATMAN in the example to the right. *Answers, page 138.*

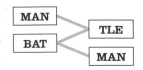

1. Very large gun
2. Rest against while standing (2 words)
3. Group of teams
4. Thick Irish accent
5. Thin soups
6. January, February, etc.
7. Girl's name that completes the California city "Santa ___"
8. Second largest continent
9. Frightened
10. Gave money back to
11. Say again
12. Possible danger
13. Liftoff force for a rocket
14. Insect in a Biblical plague
15. One of many in a typical school hallway
16. Fiddle (with)
17. Silvery stuff on the Christmas tree
18. Brother in a fairy tale
19. Storage building for airplanes
20. Showing very bad taste
21. Member of a *Star Trek* race

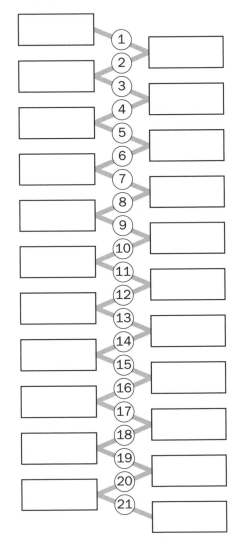

Hints: 96 272 195

TRIPLE PLAY

In each puzzle below, you can move the 21 three-letter pieces into the grid to make seven 10-letter answers reading across. (You can cross out the pieces as you write them in—each will be used only once.) Clues are given for the seven words or phrases, but you'll have to figure out which clue matches each answer—they are not given in the same order. If you solve the puzzles correctly, you'll find a two-word phrase in each of them, reading down two of the columns. *Answers, page 138.*

A									
T									
M									
F									
S									
E									
C									

▶ Achieve, as a difficult task
▶ Bathroom item used three times a day, ideally
▶ Lies
▶ One unwilling to spend money
▶ Period of 1,000 years
▶ Something to help you change out-of-reach lightbulbs
▶ Time between the marriage proposal and the wedding

ALS ATE CCO DER EHO ENN ENT GEM HEA HPA ILL ISH IUM LAD MPL NGA ODS OOT PSK STE TEP

E									
D									
C									
M									
B									
P									
F									

▶ Dentures (2 words)
▶ Poisonous spider (2 words)
▶ Religious holiday one week before Easter (2 words)
▶ Residence that can change its own address (2 words)
▶ Scientist's project
▶ Sources of milk, cream, and butter (2 words)
▶ Take away an item somebody shouldn't have

AIR ALM ALS ATE DAY DOW ENT ETE ETH ISC KWI LAC LEH OBI OME ONF RIM RMS SUN XPE YFA

Hints: 274 332 59 143

TO AND FRO

Exactly half of the twenty-four words in this crossword will be entered normally . . . but the other half will be entered backward—which is to say, from right to left for Across entries, or from the bottom to the top for Down entries. *Answers, page 138.*

Across

1 Mr. Disney
4 What pigs eat
7 Archer's arrow holder
8 Show of appreciation for a performance
9 Enjoy a novel
11 The very end of the day, for most folks
13 It clogs the roads
17 Go from solid to liquid
19 Dessert in the freezer (2 words)
20 Crazy; bonkers
21 Sweatshirt part, often
22 Some loaves of bread

Down

1 Menacing words
2 Come in last
3 Superhero with fishy friends
4 Bulb you put in the ground
5 Kick out (of school, perhaps)
6 Big battles
10 They protect your pupils
12 "That's too bad, dude"
14 Happen, as an event
15 Stood up to
16 They might take the bait
18 Simple

Hints: 39 120 204 162

ROWS GARDEN

One or two words can be placed in each row of this small "garden." The answer to each "Bloom" clue, all of which are six letters long, should be put into the appropriately numbered flower, but it's up to you to figure out the starting petal and whether the answer reads clockwise or counterclockwise. *Answers, page 139.*

Rows

A Natural container for peas
B Plant with bark
   More recently purchased
C Ultimately arrive (at) (2 words)
   Musician's output
D Big celebrity
   Workers in the Middle Ages
E Arm joint
   Elevator button
F Walk with pain
   Flinch, say
G ____ wrestling (Japanese sport)
   Kind of leaf on Canada's flag
H Tater ____

Blooms

1 Got ready for the day's business, as a store
2 Easily chewable, like a steak
3 Became more likable over time (2 words)
4 Handbags
5 Restaurants have a lot of them
6 Shows displeasure
7 Baby care item
8 Adherent of the Quran
9 Form of certain medicines
10 Ingredient in ketchup

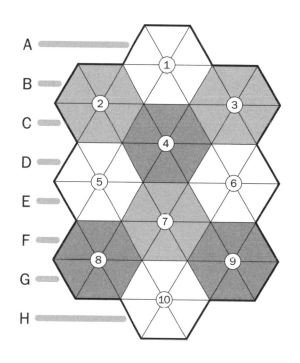

Hints: 257 197 176

SHAPESHIFTERS

In each grid, you can make two sets of words: "Short" words by sliding the two halves together horizontally, or "Long" words by sliding the two halves together vertically. In the example shown to the right, a horizontal slide creates the short words HOP, COW, FLY, and ARM, while a vertical slide creates the longer words CHOP, FLOW, and ARMY. In each puzzle, short and long words are clued in order from top to bottom. *Answers, page 139.*

Shorts
- ▶ Loosen (a knot)
- ▶ Let happen
- ▶ Add a lane to, as a road
- ▶ Say bad words
- ▶ You should cover your mouth when you do this
- ▶ City where the *Mona Lisa* can be found

Longs
- ▶ Nickname for Mom or Dad's sister
- ▶ "Weeping" tree
- ▶ Stockholm is its capital
- ▶ American wildcat
- ▶ Church's district

Shorts
- ▶ Two under par, in golf
- ▶ Large grazing animal, akin to a buffalo
- ▶ A cube has twelve of them
- ▶ Cottony bandage material
- ▶ It rolls
- ▶ Spot in a cemetery

Longs
- ▶ Dog breed with long, floppy ears
- ▶ Inventor Thomas
- ▶ Instruments on a machine that give you information
- ▶ Noisily gasp for breath
- ▶ Small pebbles at the bottom of a fish tank

Hints: 244 297

TRAIL MIX

Each row contains two answers, clued in order. In addition, there are twelve "Trails" wandering through the grid. Each trail answer begins in its numbered square and ends in one of the dotted squares—you'll have to figure out which one. Lengths of the trail answers are shown in parentheses. The twelve trails never overlap each other and will fill up the grid entirely. *Answers, page 139.*

Rows

A Barbie, for one
  Great-grandfather, say
B More than one female sheep
  "It's possible!"
C Tool used by police to catch speeders
  Female horse
D Final frame in bowling
  Small body of water
E Item in a beachgoer's bag
  Rear end, slangily
F Sioux City's state
  ____ race (team event)
G Mix two things together
  Not crazy

Trails

1 Thin plant (4)
2 Calm and relaxed (6)
3 Knitter's need (4)
4 Utter chaos (6)
5 Took a chance (5)
6 Group of words in a sentence (6)
7 Where a plug goes (6)
8 Like some warm sweaters (6)
9 Post-Christmas event, at some stores (4)
10 Animal known for its laugh (5)
11 ____ off (defends against) (5)
12 Attacked by a vampire (6)

Hints: 9 122 276

LABYRINTH

Each row in this puzzle contains two answers, the second immediately following the first. The "Path" answers wind their way through the labyrinth, starting at the arrow in the upper-left corner and snaking around until finally exiting in the lower right. Clues for these answers are given in order. *Answers, page 139.*

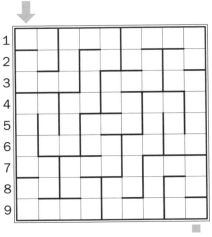

Rows
1 Famed puppeteer Jim, director of *Labyrinth*
  Pistol
2 Apple's "personal assistant"
  Longed (for)
3 Sound of a plucked banjo string
  ____ out (makes less stuffy)
4 Go bad, as food
  Prince in *The Little Mermaid*
5 "Beats me," slangily
  President's rejection of a bill
6 Fragrant flower
  Artist working on a comic book

7 Be sore
  One of the Darling kids who travel to Never Never Land
8 Linus's sister, in *Peanuts*
  Fastens securely, as a Tupperware container
9 Decorate
  Got older

Path
▶ Daring robbery
▶ Says "Look out!," for example
▶ View about something
▶ Chicken noodle and tomato, for two
▶ Famed vampire of books and movies
▶ Fish in a 2016 movie title
▶ Nickname for Han Solo's friend
▶ Long work of fiction
▶ Catching up to, with "on"
▶ Beneath
▶ Gain a point, in a game
▶ One of four on a car
▶ Joint in your leg
▶ Catch on something for a moment
▶ Woody and Buzz's first owner
▶ Winter racer

Hints: 127 89 222

SPIRAL

In this puzzle, one set of words will start at the 1 and spiral its way inward to the 50. Another set of words will start at the 50 and wind its way outward, back to the 1. Work back and forth between the two lists of clues until you have the whole spiral filled. *Answers, page 139.*

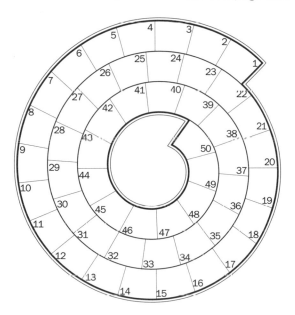

Inward

1–4: Storage building on a farm

5–8: Stopping point for a ship

9–15: Vast kingdoms

16–20: Like the numerals X and V

21–23: First ____ (medic's skill)

24–27: Egypt's main river

28–32: Moisten partway through cooking

33–38: Cousins of camels

39–43: High-tech weapon

44–46: Crow's call

47–50: Dark ____ (Hogwarts class)

Outward

50–46: Material used in one of the Three Little Pigs' houses

45–42: Unit of measurement of land

41–37: Dip for nachos

36–30: Croquet equipment used to hit the ball

29–26: Cain's brother

25–19: Archaeologist Jones of several movies

18–14: Telegraph inventor Samuel

13–11: Tear

10–1: City protected by Superman

Hints: 229 114

CHECKERBOARD

Three paths of words will spiral their way into the center of this checkerboard, beginning in the upper-left corner. One path will use only the light squares. One path will use only the dark squares. And one path will use every square. You'll need to figure out where words begin and end. Word lengths for the "All Squares" answers are given. *Answers, page 140.*

All Squares

1 Member of a pride (4)
2 Music player (6)
3 Take into custody (6)
4 Personal journals (7)
5 Changes color, as one's hair (4)
6 "Finally!" (2 words) (6)
7 Like pipes that drip water (5)
8 It's surrounded by water (6)
9 Piece of ammunition (6)
10 "Where's ____?" (5)
11 Housekeeper (4)
12 Thin plants, often near bodies of water (5)

Light Squares

1 Be defeated, in a game
2 Servings of corn
3 Part of a simple bouquet
4 Map division, often
5 Pottery class need
6 Gusted
7 Ready to fire, as a gun

Dark Squares

1 Emcee's warmup, briefly
2 Stop working after many years
3 Pass out cards for a game
4 Defeats, as a dragon
5 Grownup
6 Looks at approvingly

Hints: 11 99 246

WORD SQUARES

In each puzzle below, the five answers to the clues can be placed into the grid so that they form a word square—that is, each word will read both across and down, as in the example to the right. The clues are not given in order—you'll have to figure out which word goes where. *Answers, page 140.*

▶ Clever but underhanded person
▶ Disney movie of 2016
▶ Fake business schemes designed to steal your money
▶ Plant that builds up in aquariums and must be cleaned out
▶ Punctuation mark comprised of two dots

▶ Houston's state
▶ Lightning McQueen's buddy
▶ Make someone glad
▶ Put a stopwatch back to 00:00
▶ Singer with the hits "Rolling in the Deep" and "Rumor Has It"

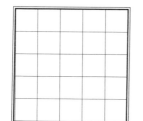

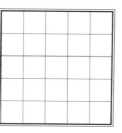

▶ Arab bigwig
▶ Genre with spaceships and aliens, for short (hyph.)
▶ Group of students in a schoolroom
▶ Midday meal
▶ Orphan who gets adopted by Daddy Warbucks

▶ Chilly and distant, personality-wise
▶ Last word of many fairy tales
▶ Lava when it's still under the earth
▶ Leave your home (2 words)
▶ Small rodent

Hints: 85 101 242 33

THREE PAIRS

In each puzzle below, fill in the blanks with the same pair of letters to make three common words. For example, if you were given S____LE, LI____T, and ____DDLE, you could fill in all three blanks with the letter pair MI, to make the words SMILE, LIMIT, and MIDDLE. The letter pairs can then be moved to the numbered blanks to spell out a familiar phrase. *Answers, page 140.*

1.	A____HMA	____ORM	WA____E
2.	AL____M	SAL____Y	SUG____
3.	CLA____	____EAK	GO____EL
4.	CH____CE	GI____T	PI____O
5.	AN____E	____OVE	PI____ET
6.	PL____GE	S____AN	WE____S
7.	SCU____	____SIL	TUR____N
8.	A____OY	KE____EL	PE____E
9.	CEL____Y	M____IT	OP____A

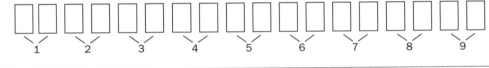

1 2 3 4 5 6 7 8 9

1.	NAC____	S____OK	W____OPS
2.	A____KEN	D____RF	S____MP
3.	BA____ON	E____NY	TA____O
4.	SAL____E	SO____H	T____US
5.	BA____E	RHY____M	TEE____
6.	EN____Y	R____IX	SOL____N
7.	M____LE	GR____H	TE____OT
8.	PUR____E	S____AT	____UME
9.	DR____S	GU____T	J____TER

1 2 3 4 5 6 7 8 9

Hints: 319 269 126 10

ZEBRA CROSSING

Answer words go across the three rows, clued in order—you'll write one letter in each triangle. Another set of answers will go diagonally down the zebra stripes. There is one set of clues for the white stripes and another set of clues for the gray stripes, but you will need to figure out which answer goes where. *Answers, page 140.*

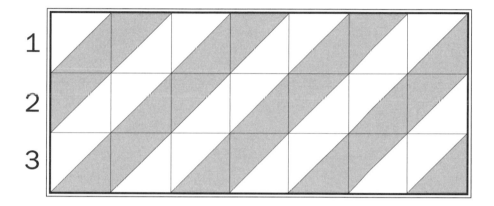

Rows

1 Eiffel Tower's city
   Early morning moisture on the grass
   Pull apart (from)
2 Mix of various dog breeds
   Quite angry
   Conclusive evidence of something
3 Athletes in the Major Leagues
   Worry (about)
   High regard

White Stripes

▶ Floor covering
▶ Snow White's friends
▶ Rightmost letter of a keyboard's first row
▶ Money charged for a service
▶ Exercise that helps the abs (hyph.)

Gray Stripes

▶ Makes noise like an owl
▶ Roman 1,000
▶ Animal represented by the constellation Aries
▶ Employee at a newspaper or magazine
▶ Almost fall over

Hints: 152 100 180 191

GOTTA SPLIT

The clues in this puzzle have split! The list on the left shows the first half of every clue. The list on the right shows all of the second halves. Figure out which halves go together. When you've properly put together a clue, add up the numbers in each part. The sum matches a number in the grid, which is where the answer should be placed. *Answers, page 141.*

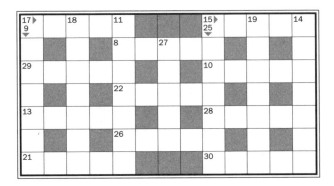

	First Half		Second Half
1	Leafy green	1	A small fee
2	Religious leader	2	Deer
3	City known as	3	Help you solve something
4	Nut of	4	Around town
5	Mythical creature	5	Down the mountain
6	Topping for	6	At a synagogue
7	Bunch of small chores	7	Business representative
8	More than one baby	8	Vegetable
9	Come back	9	An oak tree
10	Thirty	10	Hit by a playground ball
11	Get eaten away	11	Spaghetti
12	Without any	12	Slippery
13	Baker's	13	With a horn
14	Punished with	14	Product
15	Movie star's	15	Divided in half
16	Avoid getting	16	"The Big Apple" (2 words)
17	Even more	17	By wind or rain
18	Nudges that	18	Clothing

Hints: 271 32 258

SHOPPING LIST

I like to turn my shopping list into a puzzle. Can you fit the 25 foods listed below into the grid? There will be one food per row, always reading across. Letters in the larger areas will be shared by more than one food, as demonstrated at right, where SAMPLE and EXAMPLE share their final five letters. *Answers, page 141.*

BANANAS · BEANS · BREAD · BUTTER · CANDY · CELERY · CEREAL · FLOUR · GRAPES · JUICE · KETCHUP · LETTUCE · MUSTARD · OATMEAL · ORANGES · PASTA · PEACHES · PEARS · RICE · SALSA · SAUCE · SODA · SUGAR · WATER · YOGURT

Hints: 139 40

PACKING CRATES

Two words will go in each row of this grid, clued in order. Another set of words can be found in the fifteen "Crates," always reading row by row, as demonstrated by the examples to the right. Can you pack the crates with all the right answers? *Answers, page 141.*

S	A
M	P
L	E

S	A	M
P	L	E

Rows

1   In grammar, a word ending in "-ing"
    Sitting on
2   Highway division
    Telephone's noisemaker
3   Red addition to many salads
    Relaxing vacation destinations
4   Misbehave (2 words)
    Like winters in the Arctic Circle
5   Most cars carry a spare one
    Reach, as a goal
6   Part of a three-piece suit
    Even more sore
7   Trees that give us syrup
    Character who sings "Let It Go"
8   Los Angeles basketball team
    Strike with your foot
9   Strong drink made from grapes
    Stay around awhile

Crates

a   Italian for "ice cream"
b   Track meet participant
c   Seeing each other romantically
d   Dramatic works that are sung
e   Not childish
f   Tuxedo accessory (2 words)
g   Rival city of Athens, in ancient Greece
h   Busy; on the go
i   Black eye, in slang
j   Paper clip alternative
k   Sculptor's tool
l   Small African nation near Zambia
m   Football player who brings down the quarterback
n   Unpopped piece of popcorn
o   Going downhill fast, in a way

Hints: 43 259 140 82

ALPHABET SOUP

You can place one letter in each shaded square to make a word of at least six letters reading across. Each letter of the alphabet will be used exactly once. Some of the letters in each row will not be used in that row's word. For example, in the first row you can place the letter K to make the word NAPKIN. Can you find the other 25 words? Some letters can go in more than one space, but there's only one way to place all of the letters. *Answers, page 141.*

A B C D E F G H I J K̸ L M N O P Q R S T U V W X Y Z

A	S	N	A	P	K	I	N	C	L	E
S	T	R	U	M		R	E	L	L	A
R	E	C	R	Y		T	A	L	P	S
B	O	U	T	I		U	E	L	T	O
R	O	N	D	E		E	L	O	P	A
T	I	G	R	A		F	I	T	I	C
P	O	R	C	U		I	N	E	R	T
R	E	B	O	X		G	E	N	E	L
P	A	U	T	O		R	A	P	H	E
B	R	O	A	D		A	C	E	N	T
L	O	S	E	A		E	E	D	G	E
C	H	E	M	I		A	L	P	A	N
F	E	R	M	I		T	U	R	E	L
S	L	E	Y	E		A	S	H	O	M
M	A	S	Q	U		R	A	D	E	X
D	R	I	S	P		N	G	E	L	T
S	W	E	A	T		E	R	F	O	R
R	E	S	P	A		A	D	I	S	E
L	I	B	A	L		N	C	E	C	H
V	E	C	O	N		R	A	C	T	Y
P	L	I	D	O		I	N	O	D	S
I	M	A	G	A		I	N	E	N	T
B	R	A	C	C		D	E	N	T	H
S	C	H	E	D		L	E	B	O	R
D	O	R	M	E		I	U	M	M	E
E	V	O	L	U		T	E	E	R	D

Hints: 142 243

CONTAIN YOURSELF

You can take each word from the first box and place it somewhere inside one of the words from the second box to make a new word. For example, you can take the word OUR and put it inside the word CAGE to make the word COURAGE. All of the new words are clued below, in no particular order. Can you figure out all the new "container" words? *Answers, page 142.*

ACT	~~OUR~~	BEE	PANTS
AGE	OWN	BOOM	PAT
AWE	RED	BRIE	PRICE
DREAD	TIME	~~CAGE~~	SCREAM
HAVING	TRIO	CENTER	SEED
ICY	WAR	EIGHT	UNCLE
ILL	YES	MINER	VAIN

Frothy foam used with a razor (2 words)

One who loves his country

"Danger! Proceed with caution!"

Beauty contests

"There's nothing to do around here" feeling

~~Bravery~~

One-wheeled ride

Bad guy

Green stuff in the ocean

Small metric unit of length

Vision

He knows what you're thinking (2 words)

Do (an activity) regularly so as to improve at it

Fudgy, cake-like dessert

Hints: 80 150

YOU CAN QUOTE ME

Write the answer to each clue on the dashes, and then transfer each letter to its correspondingly numbered square in the grid to spell out a quotation from R. Buckminster Fuller. Words in the quote that don't end on one line will continue on the next. Black squares separate the words of the quote. As you fill in letters in the quote, try to figure out some of its words—doing so will in turn help you with the answers to the clues. An extra bit of assistance: The sixteen answers below are in alphabetical order. *Answers, page 142.*

1M	2E	3B	4I		5F		6A	7O		8P	9J	10K	11G	12D	13F	14L		15H	16G
	17C		18O	19I	20M	21A	22L	23D	24H			25L		26H	27C	28B	29D	30L	
31H	32A	33O	34K	35C		36E	37K	38M	39J	40A		41P	42I	43K	44N	45J	46O		
47A	48H	49N		50O	51B	52L	53M		54P		55I	56F	57L	58B		59C	60E	61D	62F
63L	64P	65B	66J		67G	68D		69D	70G	71I		72M	73I	74F	75N	76G	77K	78J	
79P		80B	81P		82H	83J	84A		85B	86P	87H	88E	89N	90F	91D	92A	93L		
94H		95E	96L	97K	98I		99L	100F		101L	102J		103K	104J	105P	106L	107G		

A. Soaking spot
$\overline{21}\ \overline{6}\ \overline{40}\ \overline{32}\ \overline{84}\ \overline{92}\ \overline{47}$

B. Place to find honey out in the wild
$\overline{85}\ \overline{3}\ \overline{58}\ \overline{51}\ \overline{80}\ \overline{28}\ \overline{65}$

C. Counterfeit
$\overline{59}\ \overline{17}\ \overline{35}\ \overline{27}$

D. A dozen and three more
$\overline{68}\ \overline{12}\ \overline{91}\ \overline{69}\ \overline{23}\ \overline{29}\ \overline{61}$

E. Japanese poem of 17 syllables
$\overline{2}\ \overline{36}\ \overline{60}\ \overline{95}\ \overline{88}$

F. First letter of somebody's name
$\overline{5}\ \overline{13}\ \overline{62}\ \overline{100}\ \overline{90}\ \overline{56}\ \overline{74}$

G. Chess piece that makes L-shaped moves
$\overline{11}\ \overline{16}\ \overline{67}\ \overline{107}\ \overline{70}\ \overline{76}$

H. Everest, for one
$\overline{24}\ \overline{15}\ \overline{48}\ \overline{26}\ \overline{31}\ \overline{87}\ \overline{94}\ \overline{82}$

I. Not in any place
$\overline{4}\ \overline{73}\ \overline{98}\ \overline{55}\ \overline{42}\ \overline{19}\ \overline{71}$

J. Parks, campgrounds, your backyard, etc.
$\overline{9}\ \overline{39}\ \overline{45}\ \overline{66}\ \overline{78}\ \overline{83}\ \overline{104}\ \overline{102}$

K. Colorful sight in the sky
$\overline{10}\ \overline{43}\ \overline{77}\ \overline{34}\ \overline{37}\ \overline{97}\ \overline{103}$

L. Every cloud is said to have one (2 words)
$\overline{63}\ \overline{25}\ \overline{22}\ \overline{57}\ \overline{52}\ \overline{30}\ \overline{93}\ \overline{99}\ \overline{96}\ \overline{101}\ \overline{106}\ \overline{14}$

M. Become dizzy with excitement
$\overline{72}\ \overline{1}\ \overline{38}\ \overline{20}\ \overline{53}$

N. Ballerina's costume
$\overline{89}\ \overline{44}\ \overline{49}\ \overline{75}$

O. Like the kid in a series of best-selling "Diaries"
$\overline{50}\ \overline{33}\ \overline{7}\ \overline{18}\ \overline{46}$

P. Turkey part traditionally pulled apart by two people
$\overline{8}\ \overline{54}\ \overline{81}\ \overline{64}\ \overline{41}\ \overline{105}\ \overline{79}\ \overline{86}$

Hints: 106 35 221

CROSS-O

In each puzzle below, you can take the letters from one square in each column, reading left to right, to make a word or phrase. All of the words in a given puzzle belong to the same category. For example, you can make the word ENGLISH reading left to right in the first puzzle, and so now you know the category for that puzzle is SCHOOL SUBJECTS. The six categories can be seen below, but figuring out which one goes with which puzzle is up to you. *Answers, page 142.*

**DOG BREEDS · PUZZLES · SCHOOL SUBJECTS ·
THINGS WITH BUTTONS · THINGS YOU THROW · VEGETABLES**

S	U	GE	OR	~~H~~
A	CI	T	~~IS~~	C
HI	~~G~~	E	BR	CE
M	S	~~L~~	I	Y
~~EN~~	L	S	N	A

ENGLISH
_____
_____
_____
_____

MI	E	VA	AT	T
E	C	I	TO	Y
S	LC	L	WA	OR
B	LE	UL	R	VE
CA	H	RO	L	R

_____
_____
_____
_____
_____

B	I	RN	HO	T
AR	U	CC	AC	P
C	TI	N	O	I
SP	RO	R	OL	KE
T	AR	C	I	H

_____
_____
_____
_____
_____

F	OM	EB	LI	M
TA	AV	S	U	E
BA	N	E	BE	G
J	RI	ER	A	N
BO	S	TR	AN	LL

_____
_____
_____
_____
_____

J	OS	SE	K	BE
S	RD	KS	O	CH
CR	I	DO	A	U
RU	U	SW	AR	W
WO	BI	GS	CU	RD

_____
_____
_____
_____
_____

CH	EA	SH	E	A
DA	O	TD	L	R
BE	IH	X	A	ND
GR	CH	G	HU	NE
B	A	UA	U	E

_____
_____
_____
_____
_____

Hints: 212 323 18

ONE TWO THREE

This is a regular crossword puzzle except for one small thing: Each box will receive one, two, or three letters. The answer to 1-Across has been written in, as an example and to get you started. *Answers, page 142.*

¹C	²LA	³MOR			⁴	⁵	⁶
⁷					⁸		
		⁹	¹⁰	¹¹			
		¹²	¹³				
		¹⁴					
		¹⁵		¹⁶	¹⁷		
¹⁸	¹⁹				²⁰	²¹	²²
²³					²⁴		

Across

1 Loud racket
4 "What you're asking is impossible!" (3 words)
7 List of subjects covered at a meeting
8 Puts emphasis on, as a syllable in a word
9 Long jump
11 Prison
12 Character who fights Captain Hook (2 words)
14 Multiplied by
15 Place-setting item
16 Someone who is full of himself has a big one
18 Most likely to win a race
20 All gone, as money
23 Player who gives out the cards
24 Unit of instruction

Down

1 One of many at the zoo
2 Come back to earth after flying
3 A pep talk might boost it
4 Hole in your nose
5 Walking aids
6 Proper amounts of medication
10 Hunger
11 From Tokyo or Kyoto
13 Four years, for the president of the United States
15 Smooth wall covering
17 Kind of music performed at many African-American churches
18 Disappear slowly
19 Take illegally
21 Loch ____ (home of a famous "monster")
22 2,000 pounds

Hints: 224 318 50

AROUND THE BEND

Each answer in this puzzle starts in the appropriately numbered square . . . but when you run out of room in that row, you'll follow the arrow and write the rest of the answer *backward* in the next row down. This will then be the start of the next answer on the list. For example, the last three letters of PLAID in the small grid to the right become the first three letters of the next answer, DIARY. The grid below forms a loop—the first and last rows will be the same. *Answers, page 142.*

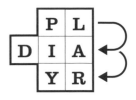

1   Dog's sound
2   Baseballs hit out of bounds
3   Eat soup noisily
4   Suitable; acceptable
5   Does a journalist's job
6   Long step
7   Cuts words from a story
8   Very short pencil
9   Belches
10 Twisted painfully, as an ankle
11 Declarations that something is not true
12 Words kids say that their parents don't understand
13 Chews on something, like a rodent
14 Trades one thing for another
15 Pancake flippers
16 Greets a higher-ranking officer, in the military
17 Oozes
18 A policeman might pull one over
19 Trade in, as a coupon
20 Cat's sound

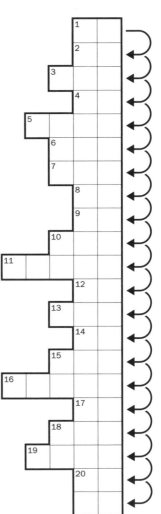

Hints: 173 203

TRAIL MIX

Each row contains two answers, clued in order. In addition, there are twelve "Trails" wandering through the grid. Each trail answer begins in its numbered square and ends in one of the dotted squares—you'll have to figure out which one. Lengths of the trail answers are shown in parentheses. The twelve trails never overlap each other and will fill up the grid entirely. *Answers, page 143.*

A	●			●	1		
B	●		●	2		3	
C	4					●	
D	●		●	5	6	7	
E	8		9		●		
F	●		●		●		●
G	10	11				12	

Rows

A Look after someone sick, with "for"
   ____ of Troy (mythological woman)
B Superman has one
   Broken arm's support
C Large flightless bird of Australia
   Nabbed
D Family-sized car
   Climbing plant, like ivy
E Protective metal outfit
   Inquires
F Tiny biting insect
   Vote into office
G Memorable happening, such as a wedding
     or a concert
   Not imaginary

Trails

1   A ruler measures this (6)
2   Mountain climber's assistant and
      guide (6)
3   Egyptian river (4)
4   Holiest city for Muslims (5)
5   Professional car parker, as at a
      restaurant (5)
6   Lizard often kept as a pet (6)
7   Cozy home, as for a bird (4)
8   Decrease in number (6)
9   From Italy's capital (5)
10 Las ____ (American city) (5)
11 Main course (6)
12 Doesn't have (5)

Hints: 210 166 232

ROWS GARDEN

One or two words can be placed in each row of this small "garden." The answer to each "Bloom" clue, all of which are six letters long, should be put into the appropriately numbered flower, but it's up to you to figure out the starting petal and whether the answer reads clockwise or counterclockwise. *Answers, page 143.*

Rows

A It flows from a maple tree
B One rising up against the Empire, in
   Star Wars
   Early video game
C Astounded
   There are ten of them in a dollar
D Photographer's request
   Bit of equipment for a mountain climber
E Take it easy
   Taking no nonsense, as a teacher
F Treat made over a campfire
   Bouncing sound wave effect
G 50 percent
   Regarding the moon
H Word between "ready" and "go"

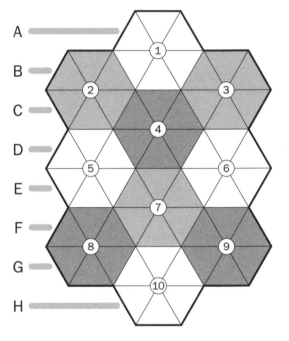

Blooms

1 Granny Smiths and Honeycrisps
2 Word on a warning sign
3 Small garden statues, often
4 "What goes up but can't come down?,"
   for example
5 Greedy ones
6 Use a door again
7 Avenue
8 Hebrew howdy
9 A ship's captain might drop this
10 Certain woodwinds

Hints: 41 307 128

CIRCULAR REASONING

You can place one letter in the blank space in each circle to make a six-letter word. You'll have to figure out where each word starts, as well as whether the word travels clockwise or counterclockwise around the circle. For example, you can place a T in the blank space of the first circle to make the word PIRATE, starting at the P and going counterclockwise. *Answers, page 143.*

Hints: 169 273 27

PYRAMID SCHEME

In the pyramid of letters shown to the right, you can start at the topmost brick and make a word no matter which path you follow to the bottom, resulting in eight different words: CAPS, CAPE, CARE, CARD, CORE, CORD, COLD, and COLT. For each puzzle below, answer the clues, then place the answers into the pyramid so that all eight words can be traced from top to bottom using adjacent bricks. *Answers, page 143.*

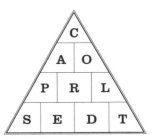

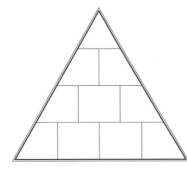

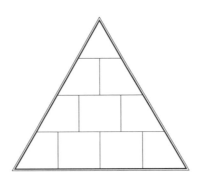

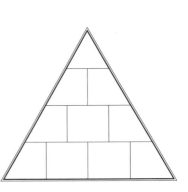

▶ Close a door heatedly
▶ It's between your ankle and knee
▶ Large boat
▶ Look for things in a store
▶ Not speedy
▶ Picnic side dish, informally
▶ Pig's food, often
▶ Theatrical production

▶ Gentle
▶ Infiltrator giving information to the enemy
▶ It grows on old bread
▶ Makes a sound like a cow
▶ Soft-furred animal related to the weasel
▶ State of mind; how you're feeling
▶ Toddler's "You can't have this!"
▶ US equivalent of the kilometer

▶ British title for a woman (equivalent of a knighthood for men)
▶ Ceases to be
▶ "I bet you won't eat that hot pepper," for example
▶ Not soaked, but not dry either
▶ Plants grow in it
▶ Projectile aimed at a bull's-eye
▶ Strict plan of nutrition
▶ Very serious and troubling

Hints: 238 5 170

78

FLOWER POWER

Twelve answers in this flower-shaped grid will be entered clockwise, beginning from each numbered space and curving inward to the center. The other 12 answers will be entered counterclockwise, beginning from those same spaces. Work back and forth until you have completed the grid. *Answers, page 143.*

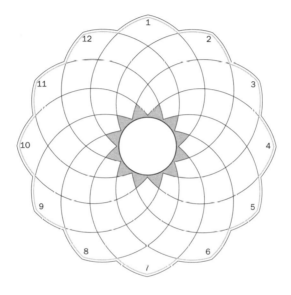

Clockwise

1. Its capital is Beijing
2. Boat requiring paddles
3. Packs of cards
4. Gently boil, as an egg
5. Slip-on shoes with thick soles
6. Much of a supermarket's produce aisle
7. Demonstrate fear
8. Hat typically worn by artists
9. Even worse
10. Group of witches
11. "Run!"
12. Put out, as a fire

Counterclockwise

1. Device for preparing apples
2. Make butter the old-fashioned way
3. Fresh as a ____
4. Tube-shaped pasta
5. Chocolate-flavored powder
6. Tiny unit of snow
7. River reptiles, briefly
8. When it breaks, the cradle falls, according to song
9. Clark's partner in exploration
10. Symbol above the 6, on a keyboard
11. Marge's husband
12. Cozy comforter

Hints: 46 94 72

TRIPLE PLAY

In each puzzle below, you can move the 21 three-letter pieces into the grid to make seven 10-letter answers reading across. (You can cross out the pieces as you write them in—each will be used only once.) Clues are given for the seven words or phrases, but you'll have to figure out which clue matches each answer—they are not given in the same order. If you solve the puzzles correctly, you'll find a two-word phrase in each of them, reading down two of the columns. *Answers, page 144.*

B									
D									
P									
G									
C									
M									
O									

▶ Big bosses at schools
▶ Book that can tell you the meaning of words
▶ Cruise ship (2 words)
▶ Five bodies of water near Michigan and Wisconsin (2 words)
▶ Metric unit that's about ⅖ of an inch
▶ Person you're closest to outside of your family, perhaps (2 words)
▶ Instrument for seeing very small things

ALS ARY CEA CIP END ENT EST FRI ICR ICT IME ION KES NER NLI OPE OSC REA RIN TER TLA

W									
I									
S									
C									
P									
F									
V									

▶ Alternative to cash, when buying something (2 words)
▶ "Okay, that sounds reasonable" (2 words)
▶ Original and creative with one's thinking
▶ Person who runs for office
▶ The top and bottom of a sandwich, sometimes (2 words)
▶ They're played on a PlayStation (2 words)
▶ Works of art carved from marble

AIR ARD CUL EAD EBR ENO HIT IAN IDE ITC IVE MES NNO OGA OLI PTU RED RES TIC UGH VAT

Hints: 57 37 328 13

STRIKE ONE

In each puzzle below, you can strike one letter from each word, and then push the remaining letters together to make a common word or phrase. *Answers, page 144.*

Example:
ÐROLL ER/C ⫫OASTER   ___ROLLERCOASTER___

1. YEAST HERB FUNNY   _____
2. TEAL ELVIS IRON   _____
3. PLOW NERD GRILL   _____
4. MICE ROMP HONEY   _____
5. VOW CALICO RODS   _____
6. SAP LETS HANKER   _____
7. BEAT HINGES UNIT   _____
8. WHEN BELCH FAIR   _____
9. SODA POMP EZRA   _____
10. BRAKE DEPOT ALTO   _____
11. FRINGE RAP SAINTS   _____
12. SCOFF BEET AMBLE   _____
13. LEAP REACH AUNT   _____
14. FIRES TACO USING   _____

Hints: 51 267 141

TO AND FRO

Exactly half of the twenty-four words in this crossword will be entered normally . . . but the other half will be entered backward—which is to say, from right to left for Across entries, or from the bottom to the top for Down entries. *Answers, page 144.*

Across

1   Write your name (on a contract, say)
4   Use your teeth on
7   One string in a string quartet
8   Little Rock is its capital
9   They make music louder, at a concert
11 "I have no idea" (2 words)
13 Slip you get along with your purchase
17 Colored part of the eye
19 Center of an archery target
20 Makes sounds like a bird
21 Picnic pests
22 Boy with a dragon, in a 2016 Disney movie

Down

1   Motive (for doing something)
2   Metric unit of mass
3   Look closely at, perhaps for flaws
4   Great time, in slang
5   ____ badge (Boy Scout's goal)
6   Put into a computer's memory
10 Astronomical event where, for instance, the sun is blocked by the moon
12 Safe to consume
14 Home to the Great Pyramids and the Sphinx
15 Walkway in a theater or an airplane
16 Dirty, untidy clutter
18 Corrode, as old metal

Hints: 65 327 284 16

RIDDLE IN THE MIDDLE

Well, it's not the riddle that's in the middle—it's the *answer* to the riddle. You can scramble the five letters to the left of each row, plus two more letters that you must determine, to make the seven-letter answer to that row's clue. The two letters you add will go into the circled spaces in each row. Taken in order row by row, these circled letters will spell out the answer to the puzzle's riddle. *Answers, page 144.*

Riddle #1: What did the dancer get for winning the dance contest?

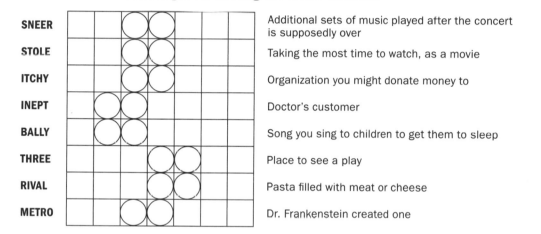

			Clue
SNEER			Additional sets of music played after the concert is supposedly over
STOLE			Taking the most time to watch, as a movie
ITCHY			Organization you might donate money to
INEPT			Doctor's customer
BALLY			Song you sing to children to get them to sleep
THREE			Place to see a play
RIVAL			Pasta filled with meat or cheese
METRO			Dr. Frankenstein created one

Riddle #2: What did the master baker say when presented with a particularly tough challenge?

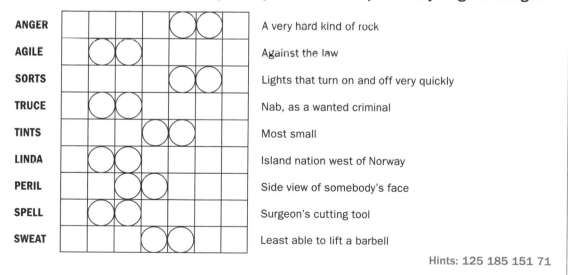

			Clue
ANGER			A very hard kind of rock
AGILE			Against the law
SORTS			Lights that turn on and off very quickly
TRUCE			Nab, as a wanted criminal
TINTS			Most small
LINDA			Island nation west of Norway
PERIL			Side view of somebody's face
SPELL			Surgeon's cutting tool
SWEAT			Least able to lift a barbell

Hints: 125 185 151 71

TWO BY TWO

In each puzzle, you can place the nine pairs of letters into the grid to make nine words—four reading across and five reading down. Pieces should not be rotated or flipped. Clues are given for the nine words in each puzzle, but you'll have to figure out where each answer should be placed. *Answers, page 145.*

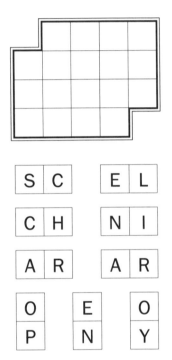

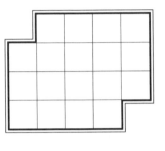

- ▶ Enjoy a book
- ▶ Lover of Juliet
- ▶ Not go straight, as a road
- ▶ One bone of several in a "cage"
- ▶ Pixar movie set in Radiator Springs
- ▶ "Send help!"
- ▶ Thoughts
- ▶ What a programmer writes
- ▶ Word at the end of a prayer

- ▶ Farmer's harvest
- ▶ Frighten
- ▶ Grown-up chick
- ▶ "Ouch!" from a dog
- ▶ ____ sauce (Chinese food condiment)
- ▶ St. Louis has a famous one
- ▶ Teenager's skin problem
- ▶ A train travels on one
- ▶ Vegetable that might cause you to tear up

Hints: 253 135

CHECKERBOARD

Three paths of words will spiral their way into the center of this checkerboard, beginning in the upper-left corner. One path will use only the light squares. One path will use only the dark squares. And one path will use every square. You'll need to figure out where words begin and end. Word lengths for the "All Squares" answers are given. *Answers, page 145.*

All Squares
1   Interlaced lengths of long hair (6)
2   Birds that fly in a V formation (5)
3   "You did a great job!" for example (6)
4   Old movie comedian Groucho (4)
5   Being from another planet (5)
6   Fruity frozen dessert (6)
7   Pecans, almonds, etc. (4)
8   The World _____ (annual sporting event) (6)
9   Most like the color of the sky (6)
10 Mayhem; total confusion (5)
11 Cowboy's workplace (5)
12 Picks up knowledge (6)

Light Squares
1   Sheriff's identifier
2   One of the Great Lakes
3   Rods that spin along with a car's tires
4   Pays to use something for a while
5   Puzzle where an eye might represent "I"
6   Spanish for "house"
7   Group of families

Dark Squares
1   Sail upward
2   Involuntary muscle twitch
3   Wet weather
4   Like an angle that's more than 90 degrees
5   Small spot on a map of the ocean
6   Pointy part of a rose stem
7   Opposite of "his"

Hints: 178 200 95

WORD SQUARES

In each puzzle below, the five answers to the clues can be placed into the grid so that they form a word square—that is, each word will read both across and down, as in the example to the right. The clues are not given in order—you'll have to figure out which word goes where. *Answers, page 145.*

H	E	A	R	T
E	M	B	E	R
A	B	U	S	E
R	E	S	I	N
T	R	E	N	D

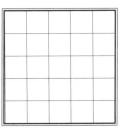

▶ Exact genetic duplicate
▶ Kitchen appliances used for baking
▶ Popular brand of blue jeans
▶ Japanese martial arts fighter
▶ Writing assignment from school, maybe

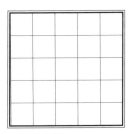

▶ Arriving before it's necessary
▶ Beach find
▶ Card game where the best hand is a royal flush
▶ Hello in Hawaii (also goodbye)
▶ Temporary failure, as of concentration

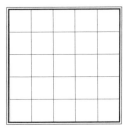

▶ Disney deer in a 1942 movie
▶ Like over four billion people
▶ Part of a map that shows greater detail
▶ Refreshing after-dinner candies
▶ Soak in a tub

▶ Go up (a tree, or a ladder)
▶ Having to do with the moon
▶ Item often paired with a dustpan
▶ Nintendo's star plumber
▶ Opening remarks before a presentation, briefly

Hints: 301 262 240 181

TWICE AROUND

Two sets of words travel clockwise around this grid. The "Once Around" answers begin at each of the numbers, 1–10. The "Twice Around" answers begin at each of the letters, a–i. Each letter is used in exactly two words. *Answers, page 145.*

Once Around

1 Superstar basketball player ____ James
2 Work together toward a common goal
3 Brownish-yellow shade
4 Wet dirt
5 Gorillas
6 Academy Award statuette
7 Whole lot of noise
8 Amazon's version of Siri
9 Dug up from the ground, such as gold or gems
10 Last letter of the Greek alphabet

Twice Around

a Bucking ____ (rodeo rider's challenge)
b Long-running Broadway musical *The Phantom of the ____*
c Group of athletes
d Island nation in the North Atlantic known for tourism
e Mexican money
f Red bird
g Look at closely
h Rooftop feature of many sports stadiums
i Wind-related last name of Dorothy in *The Wizard of Oz*

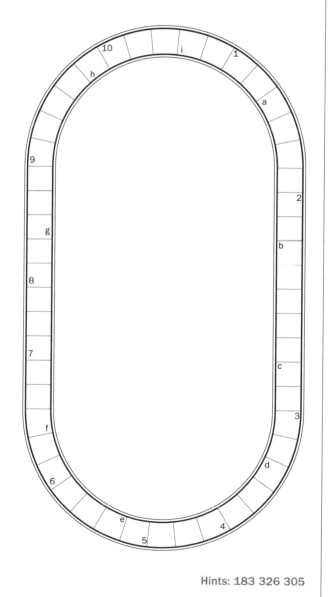

Hints: 183 326 305

YOU CAN QUOTE ME

Write the answer to each clue on the dashes, and then transfer each letter to its correspondingly numbered square in the grid to spell out a quotation from comedian Steven Wright. Words in the quote that don't end on one line will continue on the next. Black squares separate the words of the quote. As you fill in letters in the quote, try to figure out some of its words—doing so will in turn help you with the answers to the clues. An extra bit of assistance: The 15 answers below are in alphabetical order. *Answers, page 145.*

1B		2E	3G	4A		5C	6D		7J	8H	9O	10K	11A	12M		13D	14J	15F		16G	17J
	18F	19D		20L		21M	22L	23I	24G		25K	26O	27A	28E	29G	30B	31F	32N	33C	34J	35L
,		36N	37H	38M		39C	40K	41E	42F	43G		44L	45K	46J	47N		48E	49O	50L	51A	
52O	53I	54H		55C	56I	57D	58J	,		59H	60N	61B	62D		63K	64E	65A	66C	67D		68I
69A		70I	71M	?		72B		73C	74K	75J	76E	77O	78D		79F	80B	81M		"	82E	83D
84K		85N	86E		87B	88C	89H	90J	91A		92J		93H	94K	95A	96C	.	"			

A. Distance of an object (such as an airplane) above the ground
$\underline{\quad}\ \underline{\quad}\ \underline{\quad}\ \underline{\quad}\ \underline{\quad}\ \underline{\quad}\ \underline{\quad}\ \underline{\quad}$
95 11 4 27 69 65 91 51

B. Saudi ____ (Mideast nation)
$\underline{\quad}\ \underline{\quad}\ \underline{\quad}\ \underline{\quad}\ \underline{\quad}\ \underline{\quad}$
1 30 61 87 72 80

C. Event where you have no lights or electricity
$\underline{\quad}\ \underline{\quad}\ \underline{\quad}\ \underline{\quad}\ \underline{\quad}\ \underline{\quad}\ \underline{\quad}\ \underline{\quad}$
55 66 73 39 33 5 88 96

D. Style of cuisine served by Wendy's, McDonald's, etc. (2 words)
$\underline{\quad}\ \underline{\quad}\ \underline{\quad}\ \underline{\quad}\ \underline{\quad}\ \underline{\quad}\ \underline{\quad}\ \underline{\quad}$
6 13 78 62 19 57 83 67

E. Toy you play with by swiveling your hips (2 words)
$\underline{\quad}\ \underline{\quad}\ \underline{\quad}\ \underline{\quad}\ \underline{\quad}\ \underline{\quad}\ \underline{\quad}\ \underline{\quad}$
48 41 2 76 82 64 86 28

F. What a good post on Facebook might attract
$\underline{\quad}\ \underline{\quad}\ \underline{\quad}\ \underline{\quad}\ \underline{\quad}$
42 18 15 31 79

G. Cut the grass
$\underline{\quad}\ \underline{\quad}\ \underline{\quad}\ \underline{\quad}\ \underline{\quad}$
16 3 29 24 43

H. Beginner, in slang
$\underline{\quad}\ \underline{\quad}\ \underline{\quad}\ \underline{\quad}\ \underline{\quad}\ \underline{\quad}$
37 8 59 93 89 54

I. Bird associated with the arrival of spring
$\underline{\quad}\ \underline{\quad}\ \underline{\quad}\ \underline{\quad}\ \underline{\quad}$
23 56 70 68 53

J. Wander around while dozing
$\underline{\quad}\ \underline{\quad}\ \underline{\quad}\ \underline{\quad}\ \underline{\quad}\ \underline{\quad}\ \underline{\quad}\ \underline{\quad}$
14 46 17 34 7 75 92 90 58

K. Road-clearing vehicle, in the winter
$\underline{\quad}\ \underline{\quad}\ \underline{\quad}\ \underline{\quad}\ \underline{\quad}\ \underline{\quad}\ \underline{\quad}\ \underline{\quad}$
25 45 40 63 10 74 94 84

L. YouTube offering
$\underline{\quad}\ \underline{\quad}\ \underline{\quad}\ \underline{\quad}\ \underline{\quad}$
50 20 35 22 44

M. Like untended gardens, perhaps
$\underline{\quad}\ \underline{\quad}\ \underline{\quad}\ \underline{\quad}\ \underline{\quad}$
21 12 71 38 81

N. Large, fancy boat
$\underline{\quad}\ \underline{\quad}\ \underline{\quad}\ \underline{\quad}\ \underline{\quad}$
47 36 32 60 85

O. The Internet's most popular search engine prior to Google
$\underline{\quad}\ \underline{\quad}\ \underline{\quad}\ \underline{\quad}\ \underline{\quad}$
77 49 26 9 52

Hints: 17 136 119

ZEBRA CROSSING

Answer words go across the three rows, clued in order—you'll write one letter in each triangle. Another set of answers will go diagonally down the zebra stripes. There is one set of clues for the white stripes and another set of clues for the gray stripes, but you will need to figure out which answer goes where. *Answers, page 146.*

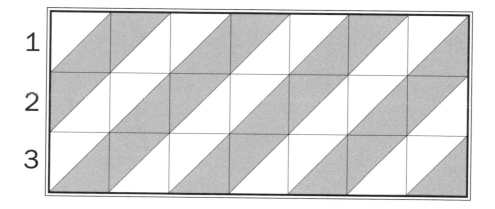

Rows

1 Man getting married
Make amends after doing something wrong
Peaceful

2 Cream of the crop
Motion of the ocean
One half of some winter wear

3 Choose
"That's a ____!" ("You can't do that!")
Shimmery stone used in jewelry

White Stripes

▶ "Can't be done, sorry" (2 words)
▶ From Puerto Rico or Cuba
▶ He parted the Red Sea
▶ What a movie that anybody can see is rated
▶ Short snooze

Gray Stripes

▶ Half of the Roman numeral C
▶ Tell on
▶ Sphere
▶ "I feel the same way!" (2 words)
▶ Sidewalk material

Hints: 14 321 233 67

GOTTA SPLIT

The clues in this puzzle have split! The list on the left shows the first half of every clue. The list on the right shows all of the second halves. Figure out which halves go together. When you've properly put together a clue, add up the numbers in each part. The sum matches a number in the grid, which is where the answer should be placed. *Answers, page 146.*

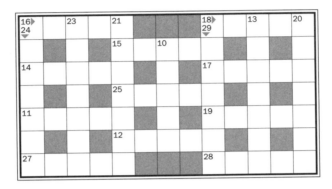

First Half		Second Half	
1	Country where you can	1	Carried on a boat or plane
2	Computer device that	2	Holder
3	Powerful pieces	3	To win the race
4	Takes a	4	In Marvel comic books
5	One of New York's	5	Cent
6	Bedtime	6	Held by a jousting knight
7	Joint	7	On a checkerboard
8	African country	8	Near the foot
9	"Doctor"	9	Moves the cursor
10	Artist's canvas	10	Skin after exercise
11	One	11	Of Uranus
12	Near-twin	12	Downhill in winter
13	Long weapon	13	Climb Mount Fuji
14	Summons up	14	Break
15	They can race	15	From one's memory
16	Goods	16	Baseball teams
17	Least likely	17	Whose capital is Nairobi
18	Moisture on your	18	Clothing

Hints: 4 108 78

SHAPESHIFTERS

In each grid, you can make two sets of words: "Short" words by sliding the two halves together horizontally, or "Long" words by sliding the two halves together vertically. In the example shown to the right, a horizontal slide creates the short words HOP, COW, FLY, and ARM, while a vertical slide creates the longer words CHOP, FLOW, and ARMY. In each puzzle, short and long words are clued in order from top to bottom. *Answers, page 146.*

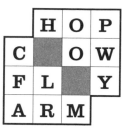

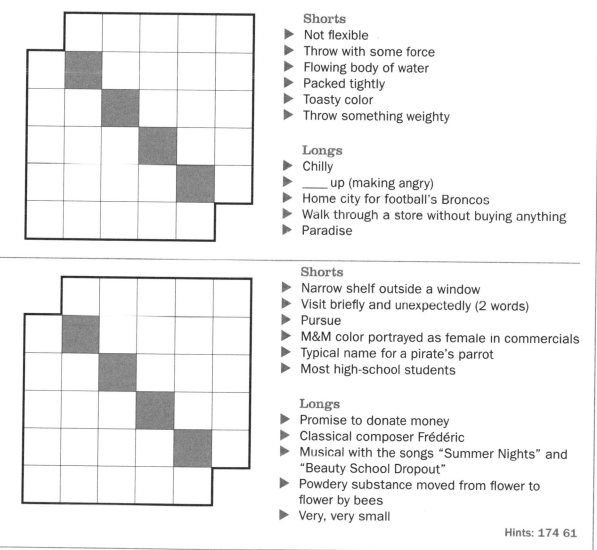

Shorts
▶ Not flexible
▶ Throw with some force
▶ Flowing body of water
▶ Packed tightly
▶ Toasty color
▶ Throw something weighty

Longs
▶ Chilly
▶ ____ up (making angry)
▶ Home city for football's Broncos
▶ Walk through a store without buying anything
▶ Paradise

Shorts
▶ Narrow shelf outside a window
▶ Visit briefly and unexpectedly (2 words)
▶ Pursue
▶ M&M color portrayed as female in commercials
▶ Typical name for a pirate's parrot
▶ Most high-school students

Longs
▶ Promise to donate money
▶ Classical composer Frédéric
▶ Musical with the songs "Summer Nights" and "Beauty School Dropout"
▶ Powdery substance moved from flower to flower by bees
▶ Very, very small

Hints: 174 61

LABYRINTH

Each row in this puzzle contains two answers, the second immediately following the first. The "Path" answers wind their way through the labyrinth, starting at the arrow in the upper-left corner and snaking around until finally exiting in the lower right. Clues for these answers are given in order. *Answers, page 146.*

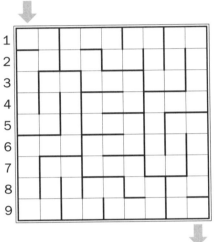

Rows

1. ____ ends (features of many a labyrinth)
   Tell the car where to go
2. Paying attention
   Shakespeare's plays each had five of them
3. Sing like a bird
   Put to work
4. False name
   1982 Disney movie that takes place inside a computer
5. Bring in a farm's crop
   Transaction between two sports teams
6. Trayful of cookies
   Word that finishes a prayer
7. Reflect back, as sound waves
   New York football player
8. Jouster's weapon
   Atlas contents
9. Dry, as a desert
   Had the nerve to do something risky

Path

▶ The second smallest of the United States
▶ Cowboy's cow catcher
▶ Adam's second-born
▶ Eight-legged creature, such as a spider or a tick
▶ Tree with sweetly aromatic wood
▶ Spanish friend
▶ Part of a businessman's presentation, maybe
▶ Soft, delicate shade
▶ Sandwich maker's need
▶ Say, as a fact
▶ Historic general who had a "last stand"
▶ Spanish woman
▶ Lion's fringe of hair
▶ Fender bender result
▶ Went fast

Hints: 188 154 22

KNOCKOUTS

Each puzzle below consists of three clues. The answers to the first two clues are five-letter words— write these into the boxes under each set of clues. If you "knock out" one letter from each word by lightly shading it in, the eight remaining letters will spell out the answer to the final clue in each set. In our example, if you knock out the R in HARMS and the I in TIERS, you're left with the eight-letter word HAMSTERS. The letters you shade in, reading down the two columns, will complete this quote by boxer Muhammad Ali: "Silence is golden when you . . ." *Answers, page 146.*

H A R M S + T I E R S

Jedi's power in the Star Wars universe + Wandering dog = The science of studying trees

☐☐☐☐☐ + ☐☐☐☐☐

Large safe + Strongly encourages (someone to do something) = Birds known as scavengers

☐☐☐☐☐ + ☐☐☐☐☐

Series of metal links + Like the number V = Head of the committee

☐☐☐☐☐ + ☐☐☐☐☐

Small, brightly colored amphibians + Shoreline = Program that tells you the day's important events

☐☐☐☐☐ + ☐☐☐☐☐

Alternative to a lighter + ____ out (eats at a restaurant) = Mechanical devices

☐☐☐☐☐ + ☐☐☐☐☐

Place of safety and comfort + Interlocking, spinning wheels = Captain America, Thor, etc.

☐☐☐☐☐ + ☐☐☐☐☐

Dirty spot on your clothes + Small, fried, ring-shaped cake = Shine compared to others (2 words)

☐☐☐☐☐ + ☐☐☐☐☐

Contributor to a charity + Sails are attached to them = They say "Welcome!"

☐☐☐☐☐ + ☐☐☐☐☐

Coin only good at an arcade + Cries out = Paintable body parts

☐☐☐☐☐ + ☐☐☐☐☐

Relax atop the water + Adolescents = Squashes down

☐☐☐☐☐ + ☐☐☐☐☐

Turns over, like a burger on the grill + Magician's bit = Makeup on the face

☐☐☐☐☐ + ☐☐☐☐☐

Hints: 7 255

HEXED

Each six-letter answer in this puzzle will be entered around its number, starting in the space with the arrow and proceeding in the direction the arrow points (like SAMPLE in the example to the right). As extra assistance, the top row of hexes and the bottom row of hexes will have the same letters in the same order. *Answers, page 147.*

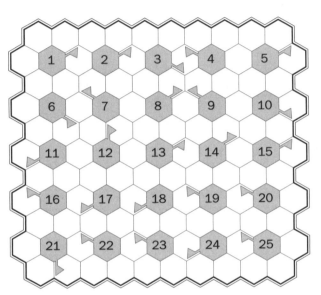

1 Orthodontist's specialty	14 Group of seven
2 Undead creature in many a horror movie	15 Tried, as a new food
3 Ate like a cow	16 What a guest might sleep on (2 words)
4 Barbecues	17 Large, flat-bottomed boats
5 Lots of money	18 Made a lot of small complaints
6 Like many cereals made for kids	19 One of six on a pool table
7 Abu, in *Aladdin*	20 The geographic center of the United States is in this state
8 Caused damage to a car	21 Lemon-lime soda brand
9 Finished cleaning something	22 Jigsaw puzzles might have a lot of them
10 Hit with a baseball	23 Cut up, as a turkey
11 Like the Tin Man, when Dorothy first discovers him	24 Sung parts of a song
12 Activity where your progress is measured with colored belts	25 Greek goddess of wisdom
13 Seafaring criminal	

Hints: 112 8 330

ONE TWO THREE

This is a regular crossword puzzle except for one small thing: Each box will receive one, two, or three letters. The answer to 1-Across has been written in, as an example and to get you started. *Answers, page 147.*

¹ F	² RO	³ LIC			⁴	⁵	⁶
⁷					⁸		
		⁹	¹⁰		¹¹		
			¹²	¹³			
			¹⁴				
		¹⁵			¹⁶	¹⁷	
¹⁸	¹⁹				²⁰	²¹	²²
²³					²⁴		

Across

1. Dance about happily
4. Silent-movie comedian Charlie
7. Invisible
8. Noisy and disruptive, as some misbehaving kids
9. Number of Earth's continents
11. Payment for an ongoing job
12. "Do you understand my joke?" (2 words)
14. ____ *House* (Netflix sitcom)
15. Ice pellets from the sky
16. Move with a bouncy step
18. Rich dessert made with milk, eggs, and sugar
20. Hermit
23. Speed at which music is played
24. Kept on the shelf, at a store

Down

1. Enjoyable
2. Flower associated with romance
3. Official permit showing you're allowed to do something, like drive a car
4. Makes a dead phone usable again
5. Push snow aside with a special vehicle
6. Hero of *Raiders of the Lost Ark*, briefly
10. Angrily hoping to get back at somebody
11. Get pulled on a rope behind a motorboat
13. Cash register drawer
15. Stylist's creation
17. "Abracadabra" alternative
18. Adorable
19. Post office purchase
21. Make a noise like a chicken
22. Bird's food

Hints: 113 149 63

BITS AND PIECES

The first column of clues will lead to a series of three- or four-letter answers. (Three-letter answers go in the gray boxes and four-letter answers in the white boxes.) You can use the letters in any two neighboring boxes—along with an additional letter, which you must determine—to spell the eight-letter word clued on the right. For example, if your three-letter word was SIP, and your four-letter word was RUST, you could mix them with an additional A to make the word UPSTAIRS. The letters you add will spell your reward, reading down. *Answers, page 147.*

SIP	
RUST	A UPSTAIRS

Clues (left)	Clues (right)
One half of a pair of pants	Most tender and kind
The circus's "big top," basically	Drink that counteracts a poison
Give help to	Drawings in a geometry textbook
Some dust cloths	Insufficient amount of something
Sizzling	Prizes for some tournament winners
Ready to eat, as an apple	Do repeatedly in order to improve
Perform onstage	One-half, for example
The I of FYI, briefly	Large decoration with jets of water
Pecan or almond	Outbursts of temper, as from a child
"Darn it!"	Take away from a larger number
Use a knife	Least straight, as hair
Lift into the air	Grow in number
Is able to	Meal between two slices of bread
Fervent hope	Carnival attraction with strange performers
Certain ground cover	"Yield" or "Stop" (2 words)
Cloudburst	Like swinging in a hammock, say
_____ Luthor, Superman's enemy	Searches through, as uncharted territory
Hammock material	

Hints: 167 26

HALF AND HALF

In this puzzle, you'll spell a series of six-letter words, with half the letters in one box and half in another. Each pair of boxes connected by a line will spell the word clued by that line's number. All words read from left to right. The first and last boxes in the chain will contain the same letters, as with MANTLE, BATTLE, and BATMAN in the example to the right. *Answers, page 148.*

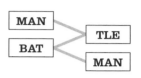

1   Satisfy (your thirst)
2   Late-morning meal
3   Black-and-blue mark on the skin
4   Express admiration for
5   Move with high, springy steps
6   Behave like a rubber ball
7   Purchased
8   Camelot figure
9   Silverware items
10   Cemetery sights
11   Allows (permission)
12   Jeers at with insulting remarks
13   The sign of the bull, on the zodiac
14   Large group of singers
15   Decide between options
16   Sullen and sad
17   Tasty tidbit
18   Animal that goes "pop!," according to a kids' song
19   Tool for fighting
20   Like some easy-to-wear ties (2 words)
21   Tight-knit group of friends

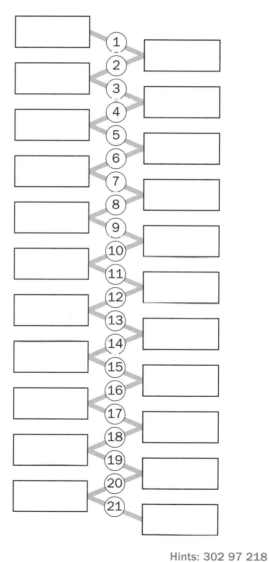

Hints: 302 97 218

SPIRAL

In this puzzle, one set of words will start at the 1 and spiral its way inward to the 50. Another set of words will start at the 50 and wind its way outward, back to the 1. Work back and forth between the two lists of clues until you have the whole spiral filled. *Answers, page 148.*

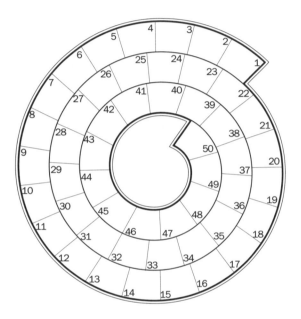

Inward

1–4: Sandwich shop

5–8: One sister from *Frozen*

9–12: The other sister from *Frozen*

13–17: Makes secure, as a door

18–23: The clothing you wear

24–29: Interfere with something that isn't your business

30–35: Language native to Israel

36–40: Ask the waiter for food

41–45: Bright light shot from a gun, during emergencies

46–50: Makes a scarf, say

Outward

50–44: Troublemaker ("You little ____!")

43–38: Batman's butler

37–33: Person using oars

32–27: Gazed at something impressive

26–20: Point off for bad behavior

19–16: Item on a to-do list

15–11: Certain sodas

10–7: Tilt somewhat to one side

6–1: Did perfectly, in slang

Hints: 68 110 23

RIDING THE WAVES

Answers follow two paths in this grid—two answers will go into each row, and two answers will go into each of the zigzagging "Waves." You'll have to determine where one answer ends and the next one begins. When the grid is complete, the gray spaces at the very top and bottom of the grid will spell out an appropriate word. *Answers, page 148.*

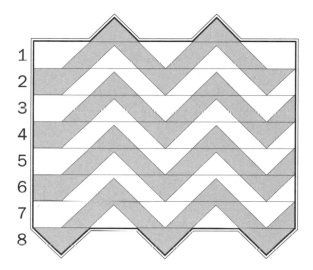

Rows

1 Sweater-maker's need
   Entire
2 Walt Whitman or Robert Frost, notably
   Parts of teapots
3 Small, colorful songbird
   Several musical notes played at once
4 Geeky one
   Feels jealous
5 The capital of Japan
   Bring into one's home, as a new pet
6 Boyfriend/girlfriend outing
   "Hard" apple drinks
7 Grassy expanses
   Froth

Waves

2 Chess players have eight of them
   "Stop!"
3 Back and ____
   Puts juice into a glass
4 Sibling's daughter
   Made a noise like a dove
5 "Cord" in the body that attaches muscle
      to bone
   What you shake to keep a Hula-Hoop going
6 Marlin and Nemo's friend
   Leap about energetically
7 Counterfeited
   Creative thoughts
8 Names of books
   Where a college student might live

Hints: 69 129

PACKING CRATES

Two words will go in each row of this grid, clued in order. Another set of words can be found in the fifteen "Crates," always reading row by row, as demonstrated by the examples to the right. Can you pack the crates with all the right answers? *Answers, page 148.*

Rows

1 Hive dwellers
  One dozen
2 Covered in a thin layer
  Makes a mistake
3 Intended (to say)
  Musical instruments akin to clarinets
4 Make small improvements to your
    appearance
  Slang for "top-notch"
5 Shape that's not quite round
  Distance from one point to another
6 Go into a room
  Say "Go, team!"
7 Round number?
  Close up again, as a storage container in
    the fridge
8 London citizen, slangily
  Office machine that makes duplicates
9 What's left when a fire goes out
  Homes in the treetops

Crates

a Turn into
b Big, fancy home and its grounds
c Construction worker who solders metal
   together with a searing hot flame
d Parts of poems
e Many a creature
f Fall over, as a tower of blocks
g Yawn inducing
h Shown to be true
i Female caregiver
j Fear and then some
k Macaroni go-with
l Black-and-white relatives of horses
m Messages warning of an emergency
n Reacts to a rash
o Says "This is what I believe . . ."

Hints: 160 196 116 254

WORDPLAY CITY

The answer to each question below is one of the American cities seen here. Cross off the answers as you use them—each will only be used once. When you're done, circle the first letter of the remaining cities. Going down the page, these will spell out something good to have if you want to visit all these places. *Answers, page 149.*

TUCSON INDIANAPOLIS

ALBUQUERQUE BALTIMORE

DENVER

HONOLULU

IRVINE SAN JOSE ROCHESTER

PHOENIX SAN DIEGO LAS VEGAS

CLEVELAND

ANCHORAGE

COLUMBUS FORT WORTH

DALLAS NEW HAVEN SEATTLE

EL PASO

AUSTIN WASHINGTON

▶ Which city is an anagram of the word DIAGNOSE?
▶ Which city becomes a healthy meal when you drop the third letter and spell the rest backward?
▶ Which city ends with a vehicle?
▶ Which city contains a five-letter woman's name?
▶ Which city contains a number spelled out inside of it?
▶ Which city sounds like it begins with the same number referred to above?
▶ Which city rhymes with the capital city of another state?
▶ Which city consists of nine letters that are all different?
▶ Which city contains a palindromic word (a word that reads the same forward and backward) for a certain tool used by a carpenter?
▶ Which city alternates consonants and vowels?
▶ Which city becomes a word meaning "cows" when you change the first two letters to a single C?
▶ Which city would begin with a musical instrument if its first letter was a B?
▶ Which city sounds like a phrase that means "cleaning a heavy weight"?
▶ Which city becomes an animal when you drop the two center letters?

Hints: 20 58

MENTAL BLOCKS

In each puzzle below, the letters in the given three-letter word can be used in all of the blank blocks to form seven words reading across. Each of the three letters will be used at least once in each word. Clues are given for the seven words, but not in order. *Answers, page 149.*

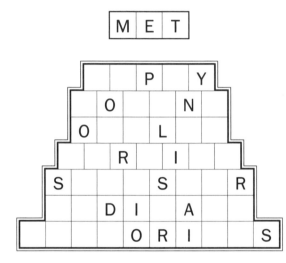

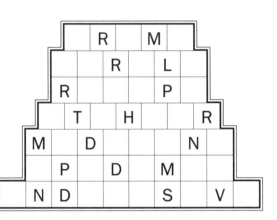

- A second or two
- Breakfast dish made with eggs
- Containing nothing
- Focus deeply as a method of relaxation
- Half of a school year
- Little rocks that fall to Earth
- Wood-eating insect

- Directions on how to make a meal
- Drug that treats an illness
- It's against the law
- More likely to get you scratching
- Round shape
- Unable to choose
- Widespread illness

Hints: 277 15 137 333

GAMES CABINET

I own a lot of games, but my games cabinet is a mess! Can you help me get it sorted out? Fit the 22 games listed below into the grid. There will be one game per row, always reading across. Letters in the larger areas will be shared by more than one game, as demonstrated at right, where SAMPLE and EXAMPLE share their final five letters. *Answers, page 149.*

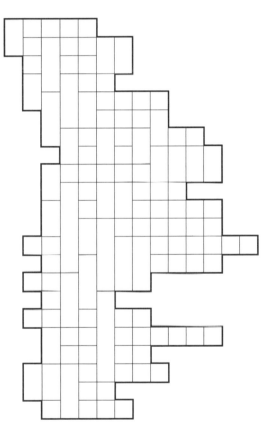

**BACKGAMMON · BALDERDASH · BATTLESHIP · BLOKUS · BOGGLE · CHECKERS · CHESS ·
CODENAMES · CRANIUM · JENGA · MASTERMIND · OPERATION · PANDEMIC · PERFECTION ·
QWIRKLE · RISK · SCATTERGORIES · SCRABBLE · SORRY · TABOO · TROUBLE · TWISTER**

Hints: 282 144

CROSS-O

In each puzzle below, you can take the letters from one square in each column, reading left to right, to make a word or phrase. All of the words in a given puzzle belong to the same category. For example, you can make the word DOLPHIN reading left to right in the first puzzle, and so now you know the category for that puzzle is SEA CREATURES. The six categories can be seen below, but figuring out which one goes with which puzzle is up to you. *Answers, page 149.*

PARTS OF A CAR · SCHOOL SUPPLIES · SEA CREATURES · SPORTS · THINGS WITH WHEELS · TREES

D	B	A	OP	P
SH	C	S	M	E
W	R	P	L	US
LO	OL	T	TE	IN
O	H	I	H	R

DOLPHIN
_____
_____
_____
_____

T	QU	MI	KE	SE
H	AC	A	I	ON
BA	EN	C	NT	H
S	O	N	OS	S
L	D	R	S	Y

_____
_____
_____
_____
_____

N	A	EB	PA	R
B	LC	C	AT	K
P	OT	L	I	OR
CA	U	CK	OO	L
R	EN	UL	E	CK

_____
_____
_____
_____
_____

E	SH	T	IE	RD
DA	E	I	D	E
B	ND	B	E	LD
F	AT	SH	N	RY
WI	NG	N	OA	ER

_____
_____
_____
_____
_____

C	I	P	OO	W
M	P	D	L	CE
RE	E	W	O	R
W	A	R	A	D
S	D	LL	U	E

_____
_____
_____
_____
_____

MO	R	G	TO	LE
AM	A	RC	AN	ER
ST	RA	UL	YC	N
W	TO	C	L	CE
T	B	OL	O	R

_____
_____
_____
_____
_____

Hints: 62 280 187

FOR STARTERS

It's not often that you can solve two puzzles at the same time, but that's what you'll be doing here. The clues to the two grids are all mixed together. The answers are all five-letter words, and each begins with a different letter of the alphabet. Those starting letters have already been placed for you. Can you use the given letters and the clues provided to complete both grids? *Answers, page 150.*

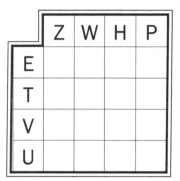

▶ A billion has nine of them
▶ Adjust, as to a new environment
▶ Bunch of bubbles, as in a glass of root beer
▶ Halloween costume that requires only a sheet
▶ Hard to climb, perhaps
▶ Juliet's love
▶ Looks through binoculars, say
▶ ____ Madison (fourth US President)
▶ Mid-sentence punctuation mark
▶ One of many on Election Day
▶ People on computers
▶ Put words on paper
▶ Someone walking along a trail in the woods, perhaps
▶ Strange and spooky
▶ Three-wheeled kiddie vehicle, briefly
▶ Wide from side to side

Hints: 234 21 266

TRIPLE PLAY

In each puzzle below, you can move the 21 three-letter pieces into the grid to make seven 10-letter answers reading across. (You can cross out the pieces as you write them in—each will be used only once.) Clues are given for the seven words or phrases, but you'll have to figure out which clue matches each answer—they are not given in the same order. If you solve the puzzles correctly, you'll find a two-word phrase in each of them, reading down two of the columns. *Answers, page 150.*

G									
E									
F									
S									
B									
D									
V									

▶ Estimated within a few of the actual total (3 words)
▶ First prize at many country fair contests (2 words)
▶ "Here's a specific case that illustrates what I've been talking about" (2 words)
▶ Man-made devices in orbit around the Earth
▶ Sport played either indoors or on a beach
▶ Villain in many a superhero movie (2 words)
▶ What you pull to tighten a pair of sweatpants

AKE ALL ATE BON EYB GEN ING IUS IVE LLI LUE OLL ORE ORT PLE RAW RIB STR TES VIL XAM

S									
G									
O									
H									
C									
W									
T									

▶ Driver who goes *really* fast (2 words)
▶ Item for backyard bouncers
▶ Kitchen gadget that makes a particular kind of breakfast food (2 words)
▶ Person (2 words)
▶ Prickly skin sensation when you're excited or scared (2 words)
▶ Simple device that helps you hang laundry outside to dry
▶ Tending to look on the bright side of things

AFF DDE EBU HES INE ING LEI LOT MIS MON MPS NBE OOS PEE PIN POL PTI RAM RON TIC UMA

Hints: 216 198 317 230

ROWS GARDEN

One or two words can be placed in each row of this small "garden." The answer to each "Bloom" clue, all of which are six letters long, should be put into the appropriately numbered flower, but it's up to you to figure out the starting petal and whether the answer reads clockwise or counterclockwise. *Answers, page 150.*

Rows

A Many a bug in *A Bug's Life*
B Movie
   Male cows
C Popular name for toy bears
   Put into categories
D Goal of a bowler's second throw
   "____ here!" ("Me too!")
E Snakelike fishes
   Famed hedgehog of video games
F Fish often found in a can
   Expressed sadness, perhaps
G Fruit in Georgia's state nickname
   Cowboy slang for "food"
H Up to, briefly

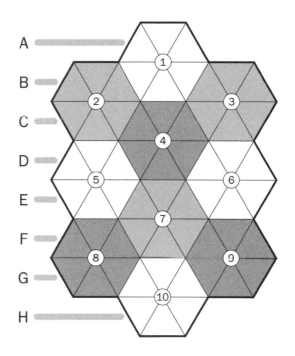

Blooms

1 Harriet of the Underground Railroad
2 Raised up
3 Casual and enjoyable walk
4 Not casual, as clothes
5 Go by, as time
6 X-Men character with the power to freeze things
7 Opposite of "down," in some puzzles
8 Ingredient in a certain kind of "butter"
9 Like a pirate's treasure, often
10 Small mechanical problem

Hints: 130 281 193

PINWHEEL

Each ring of the pinwheel will contain two or more answers, starting at the numbered space and reading clockwise. Another set of words will begin in the space indicated by the arrow, and proceed to the right, in a path that winds up and down around the grid. Lengths are given for all answers. *Answers, page 150.*

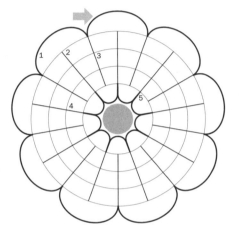

Rings

1 Sneakily delay one's bedtime (5)
   Astonish into silence (4)
2 ____ throat (common malady) (5)
   ". . . or ____!" (end of a threat) (4)
   Emit gentle light (4)
   Copy by drawing over (5)
3 Tall storage buildings on a farm (5)
   Vanilla ____ (ice cream ingredient) (4)
   Giant body of water (5)
   Inedible part of a donut (4)
4 Useful device often found in a kitchen
      drawer (9, 2 words)
   Baby's bed (4)
   Author of many fables (5)
5 Is unable to (4)
   One who likes to argue online (5)

Path

▶ Three-base hit, in baseball (6)
▶ Big jump (4)
▶ Starting word of many a fairy tale (4)
▶ Exchange for money (4)
▶ Metal in many a kid's mouth (6)
▶ Becoming educated in (8)
▶ Messy one (4)
▶ Mexican meal in a crunchy shell (4)
▶ Sound like a bird (5)
▶ Second-largest planet in the solar
   system (6)
▶ Child with no parents (6)
▶ Chocolate powder (5)
▶ Reduce (6)
▶ Unable to find one's way home (4)

Hints: 292 320 88

TO AND FRO

Exactly half of the twenty-four words in this crossword will be entered normally . . . but the other half will be entered backward—which is to say, from right to left for Across entries, or from the bottom to the top for Down entries. *Answers, page 151.*

Across

1 The gender of all bright red cardinals
4 Sheet of glass
7 "House" for a car
8 Easily broken; fragile
9 What connects a tire swing to a tree
11 When the water is furthest away from the shoreline (2 words)
13 Shrimp, fish, etc., in a restaurant
17 Stately, shade-giving trees
19 Where you might put money, in a vending machine (2 words)
20 Pay no attention to
21 Say "I'm tired!" without words
22 Stretch across, as a bridge

Down

1 Yell really loud
2 Car
3 February 29, every four years (2 words)
4 Wall coating, often
5 Atlantic or Pacific
6 Sharp part of a razor blade
10 Feather-filled items on the bed
12 Use your ears
14 Used a pen
15 Comical
16 Head-to-shoulders connector
18 Teeny, tiny bit of matter

Hints: 288 316 145 213

WORD SQUARES

In each puzzle below, the five answers to the clues can be placed into the grid so that they form a word square—that is, each word will read both across and down, as in the example to the right. The clues are not given in order—you'll have to figure out which word goes where. *Answers, page 151.*

H	E	A	R	T
E	M	B	E	R
A	B	U	S	E
R	E	S	I	N
T	R	E	N	D

▶ Book of maps
▶ "Get lost!"
▶ Large wooden box used for shipping
▶ Sloppy
▶ What trains ride on

▶ Astonish
▶ Good scent, as in a bakery
▶ Narrow man-made waterway (a famous one is in Panama)
▶ Some cakes have more than one
▶ "You're kidding!" (2 words)

▶ Get-five-in-a-row game
▶ Having no one else around
▶ Name of Disney's "Little Mermaid"
▶ ____ the Hutt (Star Wars villain)
▶ Start

▶ "Action words," in grammar
▶ Like umbrella weather
▶ More tricky
▶ Online message
▶ Overindulge (in eating, or watching TV, etc.)

Hints: 155 60 83 186

A LITTLE SOMETHING EXTRA

You can add a letter of the alphabet to each of the boldface words shown below, and then scramble to make an answer to one of the clues at the bottom of the page. For example, ACORN plus the letter Y can be scrambled to make the word CRAYON, the answer to clue 8 ("Child's drawing utensil"). Write the new word in the appropriate box, then cross out the letter you added—a letter will not be used more than once. As additional assistance, the 26 clues are presented in alphabetical order by their answers. *Answers, page 151.*

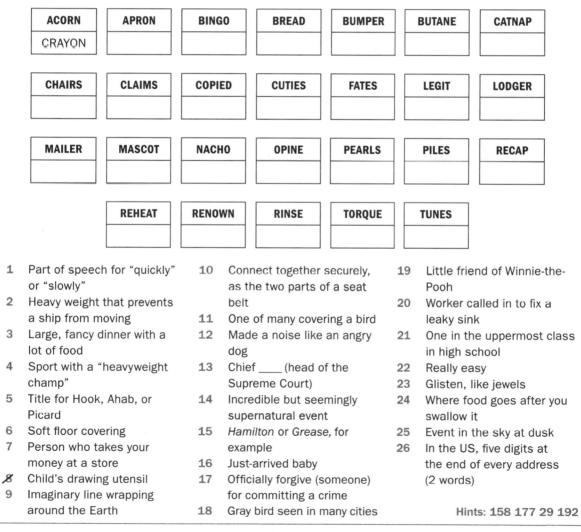

A B C D E F G H I J K L M N O P Q R S T U V W X Y̶ Z

ACORN	APRON	BINGO	BREAD	BUMPER	BUTANE	CATNAP
CRAYON						

CHAIRS	CLAIMS	COPIED	CUTIES	FATES	LEGIT	LODGER

MAILER	MASCOT	NACHO	OPINE	PEARLS	PILES	RECAP

REHEAT	RENOWN	RINSE	TORQUE	TUNES

1 Part of speech for "quickly" or "slowly"
2 Heavy weight that prevents a ship from moving
3 Large, fancy dinner with a lot of food
4 Sport with a "heavyweight champ"
5 Title for Hook, Ahab, or Picard
6 Soft floor covering
7 Person who takes your money at a store
8̶ Child's drawing utensil
9 Imaginary line wrapping around the Earth
10 Connect together securely, as the two parts of a seat belt
11 One of many covering a bird
12 Made a noise like an angry dog
13 Chief ____ (head of the Supreme Court)
14 Incredible but seemingly supernatural event
15 *Hamilton* or *Grease*, for example
16 Just-arrived baby
17 Officially forgive (someone) for committing a crime
18 Gray bird seen in many cities
19 Little friend of Winnie-the-Pooh
20 Worker called in to fix a leaky sink
21 One in the uppermost class in high school
22 Really easy
23 Glisten, like jewels
24 Where food goes after you swallow it
25 Event in the sky at dusk
26 In the US, five digits at the end of every address (2 words)

Hints: 158 177 29 192

Hints

1. The last four eight-letter answers begin with S, S, F, and L, in that order.

2. Bloom 4 begins in the indicated petal and reads counterclockwise.

3. Puzzle 4: The answer to "Audibly" goes in the fourth row and column.

4. Two of the clue "sums" are 16+1 and 6+18.

5. Puzzle 2: The bottom row is S D E K (or K E D S).

6. The top line and the bottom line are the same. Reading from left to right, they are E D O S A I C O C E.

7. The letters in the first three answers will be knocked out as shown:

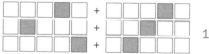

8. The five rightmost letters in the grid, reading down, are W B T S E.

9. Trail 2 is shaped like this:

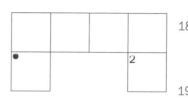

10. Puzzle 2: The pairs that go into 6–9 are AP, EM, ES, and PL, in an order you must determine.

11. The upper-left corner of the grid looks like this:

12. In puzzles 1–4, cross off the P in PICK, the T in EAT, the R in TARSAL, and the E in YES.

13. Puzzle 2: The last three clues have answers that begin with W, V, and S, in that order.

14. The answer to "Can't be done, sorry (2 words)" goes in the third white stripe.

15. Puzzle 1: The last four clues go into rows 6, 5, 7, and 4, in that order.

16. The answers to 12-Down and 13-Across both read forward.

17. The fourth word of the answer quote is PEOPLE.

18. The puzzle whose upper-left corner is J is PUZZLES. The puzzle whose upper-left corner is B is VEGETABLES.

19. The seventh word of the answer quote is TIME.

20. COLUMBUS, DALLAS, FORT WORTH, INDIANAPOLIS, and SAN DIEGO are the answers to the first five questions, in an order you must determine.

21. The second four answers begin, in order, with S, R, P, and J.

22. The lower-left corner of the grid looks like this:

23. The final four "Inward" answers begin with H, O, F, and K, in that order.

24. Answers 1, 2, 3, and 4 begin with S, A, T, and L, in that order.

25. The answers to 1, 9, 14, and 16 can all be found in the third ring.

26. The last four eight-letter answers begin with S, R, R, and E, in that order.

27. Clues to the words in the third row (in no particular order) are: "Bird of prey," "Grassy plain," "Manservant," "Crossword solver's need," "Words to a song"

28. The boxes numbered 5 and 16 will each get one letter. (Other boxes will, too.)

29. The answer to clue 7 is CHAIRS + E, scrambled. The answer to clue 9 is TORQUE + A, scrambled. The answer to clue 10 is FATES + N, scrambled.

30. The upper-right corner of the grid looks like this:

31. The first four eight-letter answers begin with D, R, C, and P, in that order.

32. Two of the clue "sums" are 14+1 and 8+2.

33. Puzzle 4: The answer to "Lava when it's still under the earth" goes in the first row and column.

34. The five rightmost letters in the grid, reading down, are Z C W G G.

35. The ninth word of the answer quote is NEVER.

36. Answers 9, 10, 11, and 12 begin with C, D, C, and S, in that order.

37. Puzzle 1: The last three clues have answers that begin with C, B, and M, in that order.

38. Two of the clue "sums" are 12+2 and 6+1.

39. The answers to 1-Down and 4-Down both read backward.

40. The food in the bottom row is GRAPES.

41. Bloom 3 begins in the indicated petal and reads counterclockwise.

42. Puzzle 2: The pairs that go into 6–9 are AN, ON, SP, and TI, in an order you must determine.

43. The answers to crates a–d begin with the letters G, R, D, and O, in that order.

44. Trail 12 is shaped like this:

45. Puzzle 1: The first four clues have answers that begin with O, A, F, and H, in that order.

46. Answers 1, 2, 3, and 4 begin with C, C, D, and P in that order.

47. Trail 12 is shaped like this:

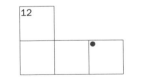

48. The second four answers begin, in order, with L, H, F, and W.

49. Puzzle 3: The answer to "Set of eight" goes in the fourth row and column.

50. The boxes numbered 16 and 21 will each get one letter. (Other boxes will, too.)

51. In puzzles 1–4, cross off the H in HERB, the A in TEAL, the N in NERD, and the M in ROMP.

52. The five leftmost letters in the grid, reading down, are L H R I N.

53. Answers 12, 14, 16, 18, and 20 begin with L, S, D, R, and P, in that order.

54. The boxes numbered 8, 13, and 23 will all get two letters. (Other boxes will, too.)

55. Two of the clue "sums" are 7+18 and 6+2.

56. The answers to 3-Down and 12-Down both read backward.

57. Puzzle 1: The first four clues have answers that begin with P, D, O, and G, in that order.

58. DENVER, HONOLULU, SAN JOSE, SEATTLE, and WASHINGTON are the answers to the last five questions, in an order you must determine.

59. Puzzle 2: The first four clues have answers that begin with F, B, P, and M, in that order.

60. Puzzle 2: The answer to "Astonish" goes in the fourth row and column.

61. Puzzle 2: The long answers begin with P, C, G, P, and T, in that order.

62. The puzzle whose upper-left corner is C is TREES.

63. The boxes numbered 8 and 17 will each get one letter. (Other boxes will, too.)

64. The boxes numbered 18 and 20 will each get two letters. (Other boxes will, too.)

65. The answers to 1-Across and 7-Across both read backward.

66. The puzzle whose upper-left corner is SH is THINGS IN A BATHROOM. The puzzle whose upper-left corner is L is REPTILES.

67. The answer to "From Puerto Rico or Cuba" goes in the fourth white stripe.

68. The first three "Inward" answers begin with D, A, and E, in that order.

69. The first letters of rows 1–4 are Y, P, F, and N, in that order.

70. The first letters of waves 5–8 are C, A, B, and N, in that order.

71. Puzzle 2: The first letters of the last five answers are T, I, P, S, and W, in that order.

72. Answers 9, 10, 11, and 12 begin with L, C, H, and D, in that order.

73. Trail 2 is shaped like this:

74. The answers to 9-Across and 17-Across both read forward.

75. Two of the clue "sums" are 9+5 and 10+17.

76. One box will get the letters ANT. Another box will get the letters ENT.

77. The three answers in the third ring begin with S, U, and I, in that order.

78. Two of the clue "sums" are 10+2 and 17+3.

79. Puzzle 2: The "Long" answers begin with C, P, Q, S, and B, in that order.

80. ACT, AGE, AWE, DREAD, and HAVING form answers with MINER, PANTS, PRICE, SCREAM, and SEED, in an order you must determine.

81. Puzzle 2: The first three clues go into rows 1, 7, and 5, in that order.

82. The answers to crates m–o begin with the letters S, K, and S, in that order.

83. Puzzle 3: The answer to "Start" goes in the fourth row and column.

84. The boxes numbered 4, 10, and 13 will each get two letters. (Other boxes will, too.)

85. Puzzle 1: The answer to "Plant that builds up in aquariums and must be cleaned out" goes in the center row and column.

86. The seventh word of the answer quote is DISORDERLY.

87. The answers to crates i–l begin with the letters O, C, D, and M, in that order.

88. The four answers in the third ring begin with S, B, O, and H, in that order.

89. The lower-left corner of the grid looks like this:

90. The lower-left corner of the grid looks like this:

91. Trail 6 is shaped like this:

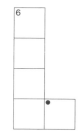

92. One piece should be placed in the first grid like so:

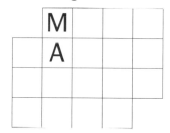

93. The five leftmost letters in the grid, reading down, are R P K L I.

94. Answers 5, 6, 7, and 8 begin with C, F, C, and B, in that order.

95. The lower-left corner of the grid looks like this:

96. One box will get the letters THR. Another box will get the letters GAR.

97. One box will get the letters BRU. Another box will get the letters SEL.

98. The eighth word of the answer quote is SOMEBODY.

99. The upper-right corner of the grid looks like this:

100. The answer to "Exercise that helps the abs (hyph.)" goes in the second white stripe.

101. Puzzle 2: The answer to "Make someone glad" goes in the fourth row and column.

102. Two of the clue "sums" are 7+3 and 11+5.

103. The boxes numbered 14 and 24 will each get one letter. (Other boxes will, too.)

104. The answers to 8, 10, 11, and 20 can all be found in the second ring.

105. Answers 9, 10, 11, and 12 begin with C, R, L, and C, in that order.

106. The fourth word of the answer quote is WORKING.

107. Bloom 2 begins in the indicated petal and reads clockwise.

108. Two of the clue "sums" are 3+7 and 14+15

109. Puzzle 1: The "Long" answers begin with B, S, M, G, and Q, in that order.

110. The second three "Inward" answers begin with L, A, and M, in that order.

111. The answer to "King's home" goes in the third gray stripe.

112. The five leftmost letters in the grid, reading down, are C G R A T.

113. The boxes numbered 4, 10, and 15 will all get three letters. (Other boxes will, too.)

114. The second four "Outward" answers begin with A, I, M, and R, in that order.

115. Puzzle 2: The pairs that go into 1–5 are EN, OR, SH, TA, and TT, in an order you must determine.

116. The answers to crates i–l begin with the letters M, T, C, and Z, in that order.

117. The boxes numbered 6, 10, and 15 will all get three letters. (Other boxes will, too.)

118. The first four "Inward" answers begin with F, R, V, and C, in that order.

119. The second word of the second sentence of the answer quote is ALWAYS.

120. The answers to 13-Across and 12-Down both read forward.

121. One box will get the letters

STU. Another box will get the letters TRA.

122. Trail 6 is shaped like this:

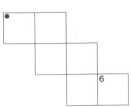

123. Puzzle 1: The first three clues go into rows 6, 7, and 5, in that order.

124. The answers to 6-Down and 19-Across both read backward.

125. Puzzle 1: The first letters of the first four answers are E, L, C, and P, in that order.

126. Puzzle 2: The pairs that go into 1–5 are BO, HO, TH, UT, and WA, in an order you must determine.

127. The upper-left corner of the grid looks like this:

128. Bloom 7 begins in the indicated petal and reads counterclockwise.

129. The first letters of waves 5–8 are T, D, F, and T, in that order.

130. Bloom 3 begins in the indicated petal and reads clockwise.

131. The answers to crates e–h begin with the letters P, S, I, and P, in that order.

132. The final four answers begin, in order, with Y, O, C, and K.

133. The answer to "Athlete's reward, often" goes in the third white stripe.

134. The boxes numbered 6, 11, and 17 will all get three letters. (Other boxes will, too.)

135. One piece should be placed in the second grid like so:

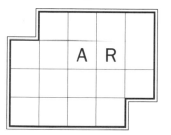

136. The twelfth word of the answer quote is COULD.

137. Puzzle 2: The first three clues go into rows 3, 5, and 1, in that order.

138. Two of the clue "sums" are 4+1 and 7+13.

139. The food in the top row is BEANS.

140. The answers to crates i–l begin with the letters S, S, C, and M, in that order.

141. In puzzles 10–14, cross off the E in DEPOT, the A in RAP, the B in BEET, the A in LEAP, and the A in TACO.

142. The seven letters under the K are B, F, P, Q, S, V, and Y, in an order you must determine.

143. Puzzle 2: The last three clues have answers that begin with E, D, and C, in that order.

144. The game in the bottom row is JENGA.

145. The answers to 13-Across and 17-Across both read forward.

146. The top line and the bottom line are the same. Reading from left to right, they are I C N I T Y R E S E.

147. The top line and the bottom line are the same. Reading from left to right, they are N U O U O T N U D L.

148. The boxes numbered 5, 17, and 18 will each get three letters. (Other boxes will, too.)

149. The boxes numbered 11, 13, and 18 will all get two letters. (Other boxes will, too.)

150. ICY, ILL, OWN, RED, and TIME form answers with BOOM, BRIE, CENTER, UNCLE, and VAIN, in an order you must determine.

151. Puzzle 2: The first letters of the first four answers are G, I, S, and C, in that order.

152. The answer to "Almost fall over" goes in the third gray stripe.

153. Puzzle 2: The first four clues have answers that begin with M, Q, H, and S, in that order.

154. The upper-right corner of the grid looks like this:

155. Puzzle 1: The answer to "What trains ride on" goes in the center row and column.

156. The sixth word of the answer quote is MONTHS.

157. The puzzle whose upper-left corner is A is DISNEY MOVIES. The puzzle whose upper-left corner is T is INTERNET COMPANIES.

158. The answer to clue 1 is BREAD + V, scrambled. The answer to clue 2 is NACHO + R, scrambled. The answer to clue 3 is BUTANE + Q, scrambled.

159. Answers 1, 2, 3, and 4 begin with S, C, M, and B, in that order.

160. The answers to crates a–d begin with the letters B, E, W, and V, in that order.

161. In puzzles 5–9, cross off the A in GEAR, a T in SETTEE, the K in KAPPA, the E in BALLET, and the I in ARID.

162. The answers to 20-Across and 3-Down both read forward.

163. The second word on the left matches to the first word on the right.

164. Take the first letter off each word on the left to get a word on the right.

165. The second word of the answer quote is FIND.

166. Trail 5 is shaped like this:

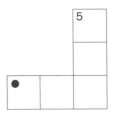

167. The first four eight-letter answers begin with G, A, D, and S, in that order.

168. The three answers in the second ring begin with D, A, and K, in that order.

169. Clues to the words in the first row (in no particular order) are: "Cold season," "Criminal on the high seas," "Opposite of 'old-fashioned,'" "Very smart," and "Where vegetables and flowers are grown."

170. Puzzle 3: The bottom row is P E T S (or S T E P).

171. The answer to "Fancy house and its grounds" goes in the third gray stripe.

172. Puzzle 1: The pairs that go into 6–9 are ED, IR, QU, and RE, in an order you must determine.

173. Answers 2, 4, 6, 8, and 10 begin with F, P, S, S, and S, in that order.

174. Puzzle 1: The long answers begin with F, R, D, B, and H, in that order.

175. Answers 5, 6, 7, and 8 begin with R, B, S, and O, in that order.

176. Bloom 9 begins in the indicated petal and reads counterclockwise.

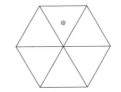

177. The answer to clue 4 is BINGO + X, scrambled. The answer to clue 5 is CATNAP + I, scrambled. The answer to clue 6 is RECAP + T, scrambled.

178. The upper-left corner of the grid looks like this:

179. The five leftmost letters in the grid, reading down, are N E C A R.

180. The answer to "Money charged for a service" goes in the fifth white stripe.

181. Puzzle 4: The answer to "Having to do with the moon" goes in the second row and column.

182. The second-to-last word of the answer quote is EXCITING.

183. Clues 1–3 have answers that begin with L, C, and A, in that order.

184. The answers to crates a–d begin with the letters M, S, T, and E, in that order.

185. Puzzle 1: The first letters of the second four answers are L, T, R, and M, in that order.

186. Puzzle 4: The answer to "Overindulge (in eating, or watching TV, etc.)" goes in the fourth row and column.

187. The puzzle whose upper-left corner is MO is THINGS WITH WHEELS. The puzzle whose upper-left corner is N is SCHOOL SUPPLIES.

188. The upper-left corner of the grid looks like this:

189. Two of the clue "sums" are 13+5 and 17+15.

190. The answer to "With added bonus features, say" goes in the fourth white stripe.

191. The answer to "Employee at a newspaper or maga-zine" goes in the second gray stripe.

192. The answer to clue 11 is REHEAT + F, scrambled. The answer to clue 12 is LODGER + W, scrambled. The answer to clue 13 is CUTIES + J, scrambled.

193. Bloom 10 begins in the indicated petal and reads clockwise.

194. The answers to 4-Down and 20-Across both read forward.

195. One box will get the letters SEL. Another box will get the letters LEA.

196. The answers to crates e–h begin with the letters A, T, B, and P, in that order.

197. Bloom 4 begins in the indicated petal and reads counterclockwise.

198. Puzzle 1: The last three clues have answers that begin with V, E, and D, in that order.

199. The answers to crates a–d begin with the letters S, R, M, and D, in that order.

200. The lower-right corner of the grid looks like this:

201. The first word on the left matches to the seventh word on the right. Can you see why?

202. The seven letters under the R are C, E, F, I, N, S, and W, in an order you must determine.

203. Answers 12, 14, 16, 18, and 20 begin with S, S, S, S, and M, in that order.

204. The answers to 4-Across and 11-Across both read backward.

205. The upper-left corner of the grid looks like this:

206. The five rightmost letters in the grid, reading down, are E H R L E.

207. Clues 1–3 have answers that begin with B, H, and A, in that order.

208. The first letters of rows 1–4 are F, R, F, and D, in that order.

209. The upper-right corner of the grid looks like this:

210. Trail 8 is shaped like this:

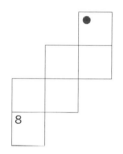

211. Answers 2, 4, 6, 8, and 10 begin with R, S, L, R, and S, in that order.

212. The puzzle whose upper-left corner is F is THINGS YOU THROW.

213. The answers to 20-Across and 18-Down both read backward.

214. Answers 9, 10, 11, and 12 begin with M, N, C, and S, in that order.

215. Two of the clue "sums" are 14+9 and 15+10.

216. Puzzle 1: The first four clues have answers that begin with G, B, F, and S, in that order.

217. In puzzles 10–14, cross off the L in ISLES, the T in RESTS, the M in TRAMP, a T in LATTE, and the G in MEG.

218. One box will get the letters TAU. Another box will get the letters CLI.

219. Puzzle 2: The last four clues go into rows 3, 6, 4, and 2, in that order.

220. Each word on the left can be found within one of the words on the right.

221. The last word of the answer quote is WRONG.

222. The upper-right corner of the grid looks like this:

223. The answer to "On the way up" goes in the third white stripe.

224. The boxes numbered 8, 13, and 19 will all get three letters. (Other boxes will, too.)

225. Puzzle 1: The last three clues have answers that begin with S, P, and W, in that order.

226. Puzzle 1: The first grid's first column, reading down, is F B H T A.

227. The bird in the top row is SWIFT.

228. The puzzle whose upper-left corner is LE is DRINKS. The puzzle whose upper-left corner is FI is INSECTS.

229. The first four "Outward" answers begin with S, A, S, and M, in that order.

230. Puzzle 2: The last three clues have answers that begin with G, C, and O, in that order.

231. The answers to crates i–l begin with the letters P, M, U, and C, in that order.

232. Trail 7 is shaped like this:

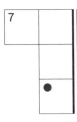

233. The answer to "Tell on" goes in the second gray stripe.

234. The first four answers begin, in order, with Z, A, F, and G.

235. Clues 4–6 have answers that begin with L, Z, and D, in that order.

236. Puzzle 1: The pairs that go into 1–5 are AS, LY, MB, NO, and SE, in an order you must determine.

237. Answers 12, 14, 16, 18, and 20 begin with Y, M, E, D, and R, in that order.

238. Puzzle 1: The bottom row is M W P N (or N P W M).

239. The puzzle whose upper-left corner is B is STYLES OF MUSIC. The puzzle whose upper-left corner is O is BREAKFAST FOODS.

240. Puzzle 3: The answer to "Part of a map that shows greater detail" goes in the final row and column.

241. The answer to "Wiped away" goes in the fourth white stripe.

242. Puzzle 3: The answer to "Arab bigwig" goes in the last row and column.

243. The eight letters at the bottom of the column are A, D, I, M, N, T, U, and Z, in an order you must determine.

244. Puzzle 1: The "Long" answers begin with A, W, S, C, and P, in that order.

245. The lower-left corner of the grid looks like this:

246. The lower-right corner of the grid looks like this:

247. The upper-left corner of the grid looks like this:

248. Puzzle 2: The first grid's first column, reading down, is E C O C T.

249. The upper-left corner of grid looks like this:

250. Answers 1, 2, 3, and 4 begin with J, M, B, and E, in that order.

251. The second word of the answer quote is THINK.

252. The two answers in the first ring begin with C and F, in that order.

253. One piece should be placed in the first grid like so:

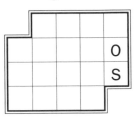

254. The answers to crates m–o begin with the letters A, I, and O, in that order.

255. The letters in the final three answers will be knocked out as shown:

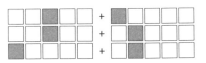

256. The answers to 2, 3, 5, 7, and 13 can all be found in the outer ring.

257. Bloom 2 begins in the indicated petal and reads counterclockwise.

258. Two of the clue "sums" are 5+13 and 16+10.

259. The answers to crates e–h begin with the letters M, T, S, and A, in that order.

260. The answers to crates m–o begin with the letters T, D, and G, in that order.

261. Puzzle 2: The last three clues have answers that begin with G, F, and O, in that order.

262. Puzzle 2: The answer to "Temporary failure, as of concentration" goes in the first row and column.

263. Two of the clue "sums" are 1+14 and 8+12.

264. The lower-left corner of the grid looks like this:

265. Trail 7 is shaped like this:

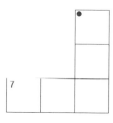

266. The final four answers begin, in order, with H, E, T, and B.

267. In puzzles 5–9, cross off the O in RODS, the P in SAP, the E in BEAT, the B in BELCH, and the Z in EZRA.

268. One box will get the letters LOR. Another box will get the letters BAR.

269. Puzzle 1: The pairs that go into 6–9 are BA, NN, ED, and ER, in an order you must determine.

270. The puzzle whose upper-left corner is DE is US STATES.

271. Two of the clue "sums" are 15+7 and 17+12.

272. One box will get the letters BRO. Another box will get the letters UST.

273. Clues to the words in the second row (in no particular order) are: "A toy mouse might be filled with this," "Guidance," "In no particular order," "Official in baseball," "Sport on ice."

274. Puzzle 1: The first four clues have answers that begin with A, T, F, and C, in that order.

275. Puzzle 2: The answer to "One who prefers to keep to himself" goes in the second row and column.

276. Trail 8 is shaped like this:

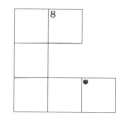

277. Puzzle 1: The first three clues go into rows 2, 3, and 1, in that order.

278. The first five "Outward" answers begin with P, B, A, R, and D, in that order.

279. Puzzle 3: The first grid's first column, reading down, is S D S P S S.

280. The puzzle whose upper-left corner is T is SPORTS. The puzzle whose upper-left corner is E is PARTS OF A CAR.

281. Bloom 5 begins in the indicated petal and reads counterclockwise.

282. The game in the first row is TABOO.

283. The boxes numbered 5 and 17 will each get one letter. (Other boxes will, too.)

284. The answers to 3-Down and 11-Across both read forward.

285. The puzzle whose upper-left corner is WE is HALLOWEEN COSTUMES.

286. Clues 7–9 have answers that begin with S, E, and L, in that order.

287. The eight letters at the bottom of the column are A, G, H, K, L, P, U, and Y, in an order you must determine.

288. The answers to 1-Down and 11-Across both read backward.

289. One piece should be placed in the second grid like so:

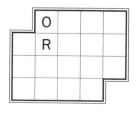

290. The sixth word of the answer quote is BEING.

291. The lower-right corner of the grid looks like this:

292. Both answers in the first ring begin with S.

293. The bird in the bottom row is CONDOR.

294. Answers 2, 4, 6, 8, and 10 begin with S, R, D, S, and L, in that order.

295. The five rightmost letters in the grid, reading down, are G D P P N.

296. Each word on the left can become a new word when you modify it in the same way.

297. Puzzle 2: The "Long" answers begin with B, E, G, W, and G, in that order.

298. The lower-left corner of the grid looks like this:

299. Trail 2 is shaped like this:

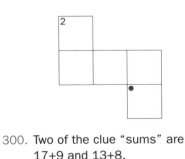

300. Two of the clue "sums" are 17+9 and 13+8.

301. Puzzle 1: The answer to "Popular brand of blue jeans" goes in the second row and column.

302. One box will get the letters CHO. Another box will get the letters NCE.

303. Answers 5, 6, 7, and 8 begin with C, S, R, and T, in that order.

304. The second four "Inward" answers begin with O, L, R, and S, in that order.

305. Clues 7–10 have answers that begin with D, A, M, and O, in that order.

306. The last word of the answer quote is RIGHT.

307. Bloom 6 begins in the indicated petal and reads clockwise.

308. Puzzle 1: The answer to "State your point of view" goes in the center row and column.

309. The upper-left corner of the grid looks like this:

310. The first four answers begin, in order, with R, G, M, and L.

311. The first five "Inward" answers begin with S, O, G, I, and M, in that order.

312. Puzzle 1: The last four clues go into rows 4, 3, 1, and 2, in that order.

313. The answers to crates e–h begin with the letters G, S, L, and C, in that order.

314. The lower-right corner of the grid looks like this:

315. The answer to "That's bad news! (2 words)" goes in the second gray stripe.

316. The answers to 4-Across and 3-Down both read forward.

317. Puzzle 2: The first four clues have answers that begin with S, T, W, and H, in that order.

318. The boxes numbered 6, 11, and 18 will all get two letters. (Other boxes will, too.)

319. Puzzle 1: The pairs that go into 1–5 are AN, AR, GL, SP, and ST, in an order you must determine.

320. The four answers in the second ring begin with S, E, G, and T, in that order.

321. The answer to "Sphere" goes in the first gray stripe.

322. The answer to "Top of a church" goes in the fourth gray stripe.

323. The puzzle whose upper-left corner is MI is THINGS WITH BUTTONS. The puzzle whose upper-left corner is CH is DOG BREEDS.

324. Answers 5, 6, 7, and 8

begin with E, N, P, and W, in that order.

325. Bloom 8 begins in the indicated petal and reads counterclockwise.

326. Clues 4–6 have answers that begin with M, A, and O, in that order.

327. The answers to 6-Down and 10-Down both read backward.

328. Puzzle 2: The first four clues have answers that begin with C, F, I, and P, in that order.

329. Write down the answers to the clues next to their boxes. Carefully compare one word on the left to all of the words on the right. Does one word seem like a particularly good match? Why?

330. The top line and the bottom line are the same. Reading from left to right, they are E S I E A R S L T H.

331. The answers to crates m–o begin with the letters E, D, and T, in that order.

332. Puzzle 1: The last three clues have answers that begin with M, S, and E, in that order.

333. Puzzle 2: The last four clues go into rows 4, 2, 7, and 6, in that order.

Answers

1: Something to Start You Off

To find the partner of each word on the left, simply remove its starting letter to make a new word. The only letters not crossed off, if you connect these words properly, spell FIRST CLASS.

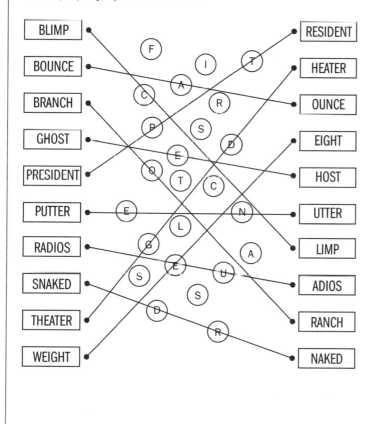

BLIMP	RESIDENT
BOUNCE	HEATER
BRANCH	OUNCE
GHOST	EIGHT
PRESIDENT	HOST
PUTTER	UTTER
RADIOS	LIMP
SNAKED	ADIOS
THEATER	RANCH
WEIGHT	NAKED

2: Flower Power

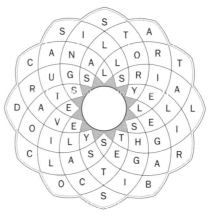

3: Around the Bend

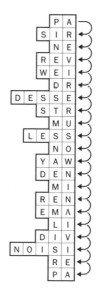

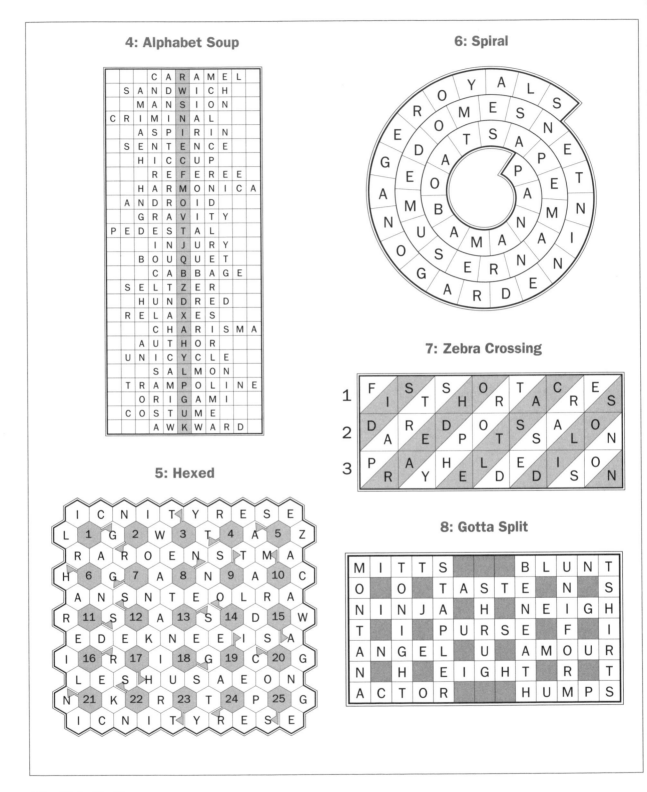

9: One Two Three

B	AL	LAD				TH	O	MAS
LOT	TER	Y				IN	VEN	T
		BUG	LE		SUN	K		
		AP	HI	D				
		YE	LL	OW				
		LUN	AR		N	EXT		
SPI	NA	CH				INC	REA	SE
ED	G	ES				T	R	EK

10: Half and Half

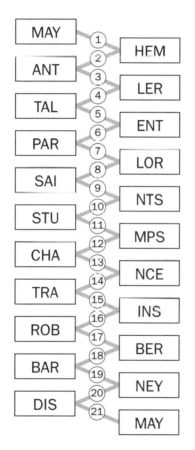

MAY
ANT
TAL
PAR
SAI
STU
CHA
TRA
ROB
BAR
DIS

1 2 3 4 5 6 7 8 9 10 11 12 13 14 15 16 17 18 19 20 21

HFM
LER
ENT
LOR
NTS
MPS
NCE
INS
BER
NEY
MAY

11: Mental Blocks

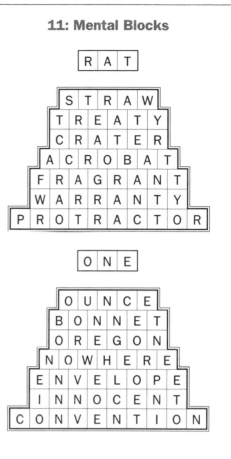

R A T

S T R A W
T R E A T Y
C R A T E R
A C R O B A T
F R A G R A N T
W A R R A N T Y
P R O T R A C T O R

O N E

O U N C E
B O N N E T
O R E G O N
N O W H E R E
E N V E L O P E
I N N O C E N T
C O N V E N T I O N

12: You Can Quote Me

A. BEHAVING
B. BRISKET
C. DOCTOR DOOM
D. EURO
E. EYESORE
F. FINDING DORY
G. HEAVY METAL
H. MENTIONED
I. OUTS
J. OVATION
K. THIRTEEN
L. TIES

"I find television very educating. Every time somebody turns on the set, I go into the other room and read a book."—Groucho Marx

13: Packing Crates

1	M	A	S	C	O	T	A	M	E	N
2	R	A	R	E	S	I	N	G	E	R
3	C	A	P	E	S	T	I	N	G	Y
4	P	I	A	N	O	L	A	B	O	R
5	G	L	U	T	E	N	I	T	C	H
6	E	T	C	H	E	D	R	A	I	D
7	M	E	R	R	Y	P	E	S	T	O
8	A	D	D	I	N	G	R	A	I	L
9	O	W	N	E	R	I	N	S	E	T

14: Labyrinth

1	M	A	I	Z	E	P	L	E	A
2	O	W	L	S	B	U	S	T	S
3	O	S	C	A	R	Y	E	A	H
4	T	R	A	C	K	E	L	S	E
5	O	N	T	I	M	E	A	D	D
6	M	O	R	N	G	L	A	R	E
7	B	R	E	A	K	E	X	I	T
8	O	U	T	S	A	G	I	L	E
9	N	E	P	A	L	E	V	E	R

15: Triple Play

F	A	L	S	E	A	L	A	R	M
O	B	J	E	C	T	I	O	N	S
P	R	O	P	E	R	N	O	U	N
S	A	N	D	W	I	C	H	E	S
W	H	I	T	E	B	O	A	R	D
H	A	L	F	D	O	L	L	A	R
A	M	B	U	L	A	N	C	E	S

G	E	N	E	R	O	S	I	T	Y
Q	U	I	N	T	U	P	L	E	T
F	L	I	G	H	T	P	L	A	N
O	V	A	L	O	F	F	I	C	E
M	O	V	I	E	N	I	G	H	T
S	K	Y	S	C	R	A	P	E	R
H	I	G	H	C	H	A	I	R	S

16: Twice Around

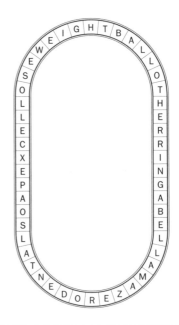

17: Trail Mix

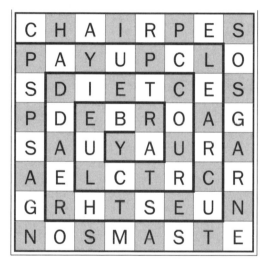

A	M	A	G	I	C	S	T	A	R
B	T	R	A	Y	A	P	P	L	E
C	R	A	K	E	S	F	E	E	T
D	H	A	L	L	T	E	A	R	S
E	S	I	L	O	S	A	H	O	Y
F	R	A	M	P	T	R	A	C	K
G	S	O	R	E	H	E	A	D	S

18: Checkerboard

C	H	A	I	R	P	E	S
P	A	Y	U	P	C	L	O
S	D	I	E	T	C	E	S
P	D	E	B	R	O	A	G
S	A	U	Y	A	U	R	A
A	E	L	C	T	R	C	R
G	R	H	T	S	E	U	N
N	O	S	M	A	S	T	E

19: Cross-O

SHAPES: circle, hexagon, rhombus, square, trapezoid
DRINKS: coffee, juice, lemonade, seltzer, water
US STATES: California, Delaware, Missouri, Oregon, Vermont
DISNEY MOVIES: *Aladdin, Cinderella, Frozen, Pinocchio, Tangled*
INSECTS: beetle, firefly, katydid, ladybug, mosquito
INTERNET COMPANIES: Facebook, Google, Netflix, Snapchat, Twitter

20: Gotta Split

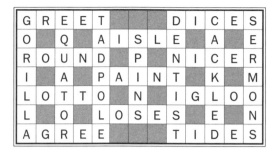

G	R	E	E	T			D	I	C	E	S
O	Q	A	I	S	L	E		A		E	
R	O	U	N	D		P	N	I	C	E	R
I	A	P	A	I	N	T		K		M	
L	O	T	T	O		N	I	G	L	O	O
L	O		L	O	S	E	S		E	N	
A	G	R	E	E			T	I	D	E	S

21: Shapeshifters

	U	T	T	E	R
B	R	U	C	E	
S	P	O	O	N	
M	A	R	C	H	
G	L	I	T	Z	
Q	U	A	R	T	

	E	N	T	E	R
C	R	A	T	E	
P	I	N	C	H	
Q	U	E	E	N	
S	C	R	E	W	
B	U	R	R	O	

22: Three Pairs

1. CANOE   IGNORE   RHINO
2. PASTA   SQUASH   TOAST
3. GOOSE   INSECT   WISER
4. AMBUSH   EMBER   LAMBS
5. FLYING   JELLY   LYRIC
6. BREAD   SECRET   SIREN
7. QUACK   SQUID   SEQUEL
8. ADMIRE   CHAIR   DIRTY
9. GREED   MEDIA   NEEDLE

NO ASSEMBLY REQUIRED

1. ASHORE   SMASH   SUSHI
2. BEFORE   HORSE   MAYOR
3. STATUE   TASTY   TOTAL
4. BOTTOM   MOTTO   OTTER
5. BURDEN   FENCE   HYENA
6. TIGER   NATION   PATIO
7. APRON   HONEST   PHONY
8. DISPEL   SPEED   GRASP
9. CHANGE   ORGAN   PANIC

SHORT ATTENTION SPAN

23: Zebra Crossing

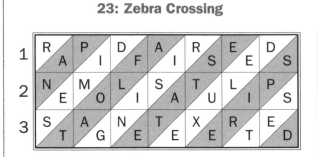

26: One Two Three

B	AS	SES				HO	B	BIT
IND	IAN	A				TR	ASH	ES
		ME	TER		WO	OD		
			RI	VE	R			
			BL	IN	KS			
		CON	E		HOP	E		
SI	LEN	CE				RA	IN	BOW
REN	T	AL				SE	NS	ED

24: Spiral

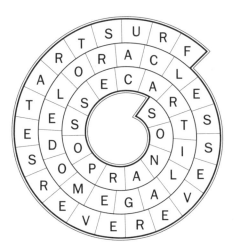

27: Word Squares

E	M	O	J	I
M	O	P	E	D
O	P	I	N	E
J	E	N	G	A
I	D	E	A	S

O	L	I	V	E
L	O	N	E	R
I	N	D	I	A
V	E	I	N	S
E	R	A	S	E

W	A	G	O	N
A	L	I	C	E
G	I	F	T	S
O	C	T	E	T
N	E	S	T	S

V	E	G	A	N
E	X	I	L	E
G	I	J	O	E
A	L	O	U	D
N	E	E	D	S

25: Strike One

1. CANDLESTICK
2. EAGLE SCOUT
3. PASTA SALAD
4. BABYSITTER
5. COAT HANGER
6. FALSE TEETH
7. SCRAP PAPER
8. BASEBALL TEAM
9. CREDIT CARD
10. CRUISE SHIP
11. WEDDING DRESS
12. ORCHESTRA PIT
13. LICENSE PLATE
14. METEOR SHOWER

28: To and Fro

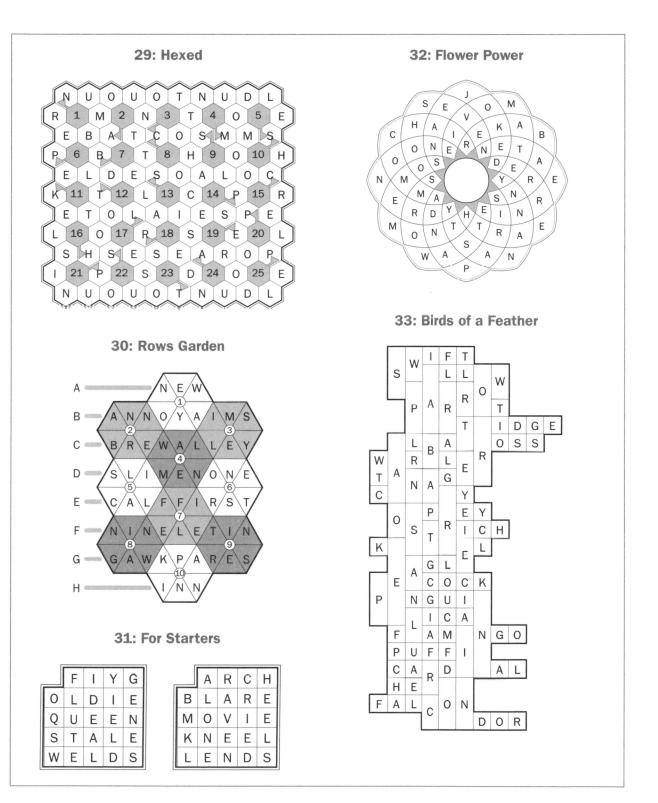

29: Hexed

32: Flower Power

30: Rows Garden

33: Birds of a Feather

31: For Starters

34: Two by Two

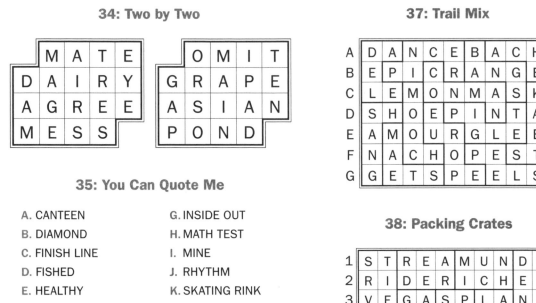

M	A	T	E
D	A	I	R	Y
A	G	R	E	E
M	E	S	S

O	M	I	T
G	R	A	P	E
A	S	I	A	N
P	O	N	D

35: You Can Quote Me

A. CANTEEN
B. DIAMOND
C. FINISH LINE
D. FISHED
E. HEALTHY
F. HORN

G. INSIDE OUT
H. MATH TEST
I. MINE
J. RHYTHM
K. SKATING RINK
L. TENNIS COURT

"I think and think for months and years. Ninety-nine times the conclusion is false. The hundredth time I am right."—Albert Einstein

36: Labyrinth

	1	2	3	4	5	6	7	8	9
1	S	E	L	L	H	O	L	D	S
2	A	T	T	I	C	N	E	A	T
3	D	U	E	T	P	O	P	P	A
4	A	M	B	L	E	B	I	N	G
5	W	R	E	N	Z	E	R	O	S
6	A	R	M	O	R	B	E	S	T
7	G	R	E	E	N	T	A	P	E
8	R	E	D	I	D	R	I	L	E
9	A	D	O	B	E	M	A	I	D

37: Trail Mix

	D	A	N	C	E	B	A	C	H
A	D	A	N	C	E	B	A	C	H
B	E	P	I	C	R	A	N	G	E
C	L	E	M	O	N	M	A	S	K
D	S	H	O	E	P	I	N	T	A
E	A	M	O	U	R	G	L	E	E
F	N	A	C	H	O	P	E	S	T
G	G	E	T	S	P	E	E	L	S

38: Packing Crates

	1	2	3	4	5	6	7	8	9	10
1	S	T	R	E	A	M	U	N	D	O
2	R	I	D	E	R	I	C	H	E	S
3	V	E	G	A	S	P	L	A	N	T
4	C	O	R	D	R	E	C	I	P	E
5	A	R	E	N	A	D	E	R	E	K
6	S	E	M	I	D	U	N	K	E	D
7	C	H	A	I	R	I	N	D	E	X
8	R	O	D	E	N	T	O	N	C	E
9	M	E	T	A	L	S	I	L	L	S

39: Riding the Waves

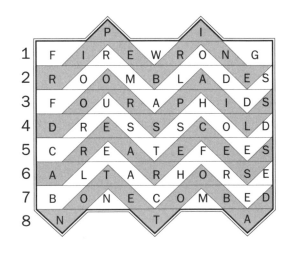

40: Checkerboard

S	N	A	I	L	N	E	E
N	O	T	P	E	E	R	D
K	C	O	M	B	A	N	L
E	T	W	E	E	T	O	E
N	I	N	S	D	S	O	A
C	S	A	I	S	A	D	N
A	P	E	E	D	E	L	N
S	Y	A	S	S	E	E	I

41: Around the Bend

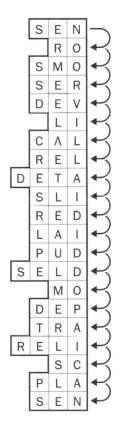

```
S  E  N
   R  O
S  M  O
S  E  R
D  E  V
      L  I
C  A  L
R  E  L
D  E  T  A
S  L  I
R  E  D
L  A  I
P  U  D
S  E  L  D
   M  O
D  E  P
T  R  A
R  E  L  I
   S  C
P  L  A
S  E  N
```

42: Bits and Pieces

ADE	Y	DYNAMITE
MINT	O	ROMANTIC
CAR	U	CAPTURES
PETS	A	POTATOES
TOO	R	PORTHOLE
HELP	E	PINWHEEL
WIN	A	RAINBOWS
ROBS	L	LOBSTERS
SET	L	SPLATTER
TRAP	M	TRAMPLED
LED	I	FIELDERS
REFS	X	REFLEXES
EEL	E	SLEEPIER
RIPS	D	SPRINTED
TEN	U	FOURTEEN
FORE	P	LEAPFROG
LAG		

43: Gotta Split

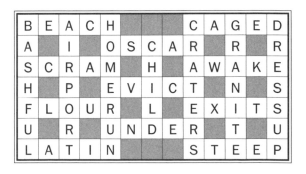

B	E	A	C	H				C	A	G	E	D
A		I	O	S	C	A	R		R			R
S	C	R	A	M		H		A	W	A	K	E
H		P	E	V	I	C	T		N			S
F	L	O	U	R		L		E	X	I	T	S
U		R	U	N	D	E	R		T			U
L	A	T	I	N				S	T	E	E	P

44: Crossfire

Each word on the left can be found within one of the words on the right, as with QUIT and MO*SQUIT*O. After you've crossed out the appropriate letters, the remaining letters spell INSIDE OUT.

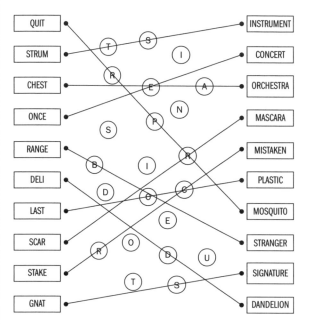

QUIT	INSTRUMENT
STRUM	CONCERT
CHEST	ORCHESTRA
ONCE	MASCARA
RANGE	MISTAKEN
DELI	PLASTIC
LAST	MOSQUITO
SCAR	STRANGER
STAKE	SIGNATURE
GNAT	DANDELION

45: Cross-O

GEMSTONES: diamond, emerald, garnet, sapphire, turquoise

REPTILES: crocodile, gecko, iguana, lizard, turtle

HALLOWEEN COSTUMES: skeleton, vampire, werewolf, witch, zombie

STYLES OF MUSIC: blues, classical, country, heavy metal, hip hop

THINGS IN A BATHROOM: plunger, shampoo, soapdish, toothpaste, towel

BREAKFAST FOODS: bacon, cereal, omelet, pancake, yogurt

46: 20 Questions

1. CHAIN (CHINA)
2. NASCENT (ASCENT, SCENT, CENT)
3. FORKING (FOR KING)
4. CLIPS (ECLIPSE)
5. BROWNIE (BONE)
6. DEVIL (LIVED)
7. INCUBATE (CUBA)
8. BAROMETER (ROME)
9. FRONTIER
10. CORKSCREW
11. SPRAINED
12. ACHE (RACHEL)
13. FEATHER (FATHER)
14. PARENT
15. SWIMS
16. KNIGHT
17. ROSE
18. ALAS (ALASKA)
19. BELOW (BELLOW)
20. HIDEOUT (HIDEOUS)

The remaining words can be arranged to spell the quote MAKE EACH DAY YOUR MASTERPIECE.

47: Pinwheel

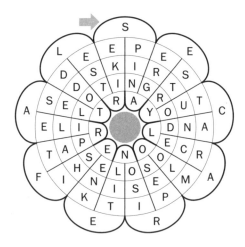

48: Cross Anagrams

F	E	A	R	S		1		S	A	F	E	R
B	R	E	A	K		2		B	A	K	E	R
H	A	U	L	S		3		H	U	L	A	S
T	R	A	I	L		4		T	R	I	A	L
A	D	E	P	T		5		T	A	P	E	D

E	A	R	N	S		1		S	N	A	R	E
C	A	D	E	T		2		A	C	T	E	D
O	R	G	A	N		3		G	R	O	A	N
C	O	U	L	D		4		C	L	O	U	D
T	A	B	L	E		5		B	L	E	A	T

S	I	L	E	N	T		1		E	N	L	I	S	T
D	E	N	I	E	D		2		I	N	D	E	E	D
S	T	A	G	E	S		3		S	A	G	E	S	T
P	I	E	R	C	E		4		R	E	C	I	P	E
S	T	A	N	C	E		5		A	S	C	E	N	T
S	L	E	U	T	H		6		H	U	S	T	L	E

49: Flower Power

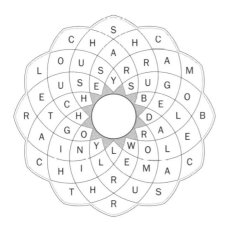

50: One Two Three

S	PI	GOT			PI	STO	L
AT	TA	CH			R	OD	EO
		A	DE		SK	ATE	
			CA	BL	E		
			D	IMP	LE		
		LI	ES		TON	GUE	
HER	MI	ONE			S	CO	RE
B	LE	SS			T	INS	EL

51: Hexed

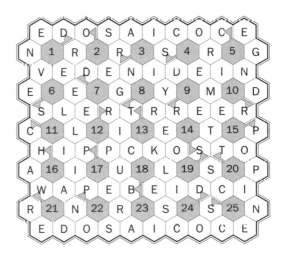

52: You Can Quote Me

A. BIKINI

B. CAVEMAN

C. DOODAD

D. ELEVATOR

E. FACES

F. FICTION

G. HISSED

H. NESTS

I. NOGGIN

J. RIGHT ANGLE

K. SIXTEEN

L. TOY STORY

"One of the advantages of being disorderly is that one is constantly making exciting discoveries."—A. A. Milne

53: Half and Half

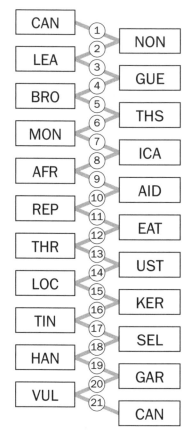

54: Triple Play

A	C	C	O	M	P	L	I	S	H
T	O	O	T	H	P	A	S	T	E
M	I	L	L	E	N	N	I	U	M
F	A	L	S	E	H	O	O	D	S
S	T	E	P	L	A	D	D	E	R
E	N	G	A	G	E	M	E	N	T
C	H	E	A	P	S	K	A	T	E

E	X	P	E	R	I	M	E	N	T
D	A	I	R	Y	F	A	R	M	S
C	O	N	F	I	S	C	A	T	E
M	O	B	I	L	E	H	O	M	E
B	L	A	C	K	W	I	D	O	W
P	A	L	M	S	U	N	D	A	Y
F	A	L	S	E	T	E	E	T	H

55: To and Fro

T	L	A	W	P	O	L	S
A	O	Q	U	I	V	E	R
E	S	U	A	L	P	P	A
R	E	A	D	U	S	X	W
H	E	M	I	T	D	E	B
T	R	A	F	F	I	C	U
F	U	N	A	T	L	E	M
I	C	E	C	R	E	A	M
S	C	R	E	W	Y	S	E
H	O	O	D	S	E	Y	R

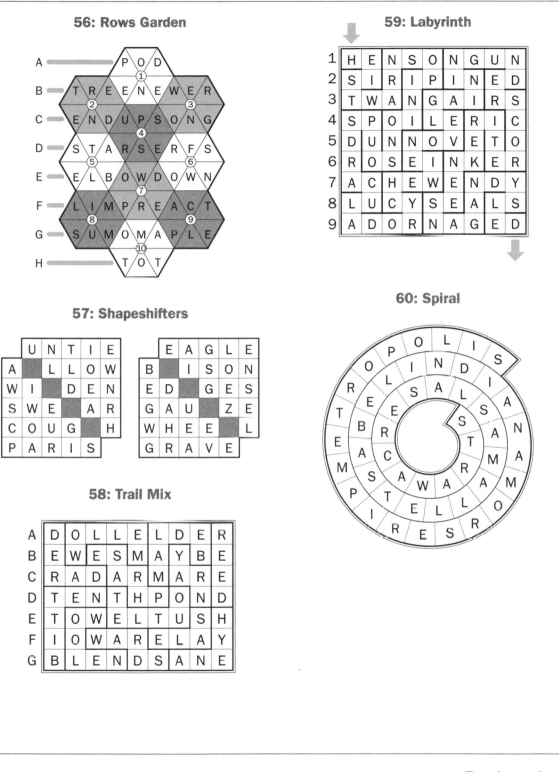

56: Rows Garden

A: P O D
B: T R E E N E W E R
C: E N D U P S O N G
D: S T A R S E R F S
E: E L B O W D O W N
F: L I M P R E A C T
G: S U M O M A P L E
H: T O T

57: Shapeshifters

	U	N	T	I	E	
A		L	L	O	W
W	I		D	E	N
S	W	E		A	R
C	O	U	G		H
P	A	R	I	S	

	E	A	G	L	E
B		I	S	O	N
E	D		G	E	S
G	A	U		Z	E
W	H	E	E		L
G	R	A	V	E	

58: Trail Mix

A	D	O	L	L	E	L	D	E	R
B	E	W	E	S	M	A	Y	B	E
C	R	A	D	A	R	M	A	R	E
D	T	E	N	T	H	P	O	N	D
E	T	O	W	E	L	T	U	S	H
F	I	O	W	A	R	E	L	A	Y
G	B	L	E	N	D	S	A	N	E

59: Labyrinth

1	H	E	N	S	O	N	G	U	N
2	S	I	R	I	P	I	N	E	D
3	T	W	A	N	G	A	I	R	S
4	S	P	O	I	L	E	R	I	C
5	D	U	N	N	O	V	E	T	O
6	R	O	S	E	I	N	K	E	R
7	A	C	H	E	W	E	N	D	Y
8	L	U	C	Y	S	E	A	L	S
9	A	D	O	R	N	A	G	E	D

60: Spiral

61: Checkerboard

L	I	O	N	S	T	E	R
A	T	L	A	S	T	L	E
S	L	E	T	W	A	E	O
E	L	R	E	E	L	A	A
Y	U	D	S	D	D	K	R
D	B	I	A	M	O	Y	R
S	D	N	A	L	S	I	E
E	I	R	A	I	D	T	S

62: Word Squares

S	C	A	M	S
C	O	L	O	N
A	L	G	A	E
M	O	A	N	A
S	N	E	A	K

M	A	T	E	R
A	D	E	L	E
T	E	X	A	S
E	L	A	T	E
R	E	S	E	T

C	L	A	S	S
L	U	N	C	H
A	N	N	I	E
S	C	I	F	I
S	H	E	I	K

M	A	G	M	A
A	L	O	O	F
G	O	O	U	T
M	O	U	S	E
A	F	T	E	R

63: Three Pairs

1. ASTHMA   STORM   WASTE
2. ALARM   SALARY   SUGAR
3. CLASP   SPEAK   GOSPEL
4. CHANCE   GIANT   PIANO
5. ANGLE   GLOVE   PIGLET
6. PLEDGE   SEDAN   WEEDS
7. SCUBA   BASIL   TURBAN
8. ANNOY   KENNEL   PENNE
9. CELERY   MERIT   OPERA

STAR-SPANGLED BANNER

1. NACHO   SHOOK   WHOOPS
2. AWAKEN   DWARF   SWAMP
3. BABOON   EBONY   TABOO
4. SALUTE   SOUTH   TUTUS
5. BATHE   RHYTHM   TEETH
6. ENEMY   REMIX   SOLEMN
7. MAPLE   GRAPH   TEAPOT
8. PURPLE   SPLAT   PLUME
9. DRESS   GUEST   JESTER

HOW ABOUT THEM APPLES

64: Zebra Crossing

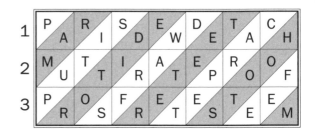

65: Gotta Split

S	A	U	C	E				F	I	N	E	D
P		N		R	A	B	B	I	E		E		E
I	C	I	E	R		R		F	A	W	N	S
N		C		A	G	E	N	T		Y		C
A	C	O	R	N		A		E	R	O	D	E
C		R		D	O	D	G	E		R		N
H	I	N	T	S				N	A	K	E	D

66: Shopping List

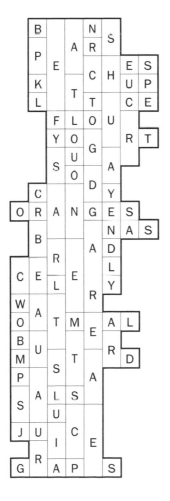

67: Packing Crates

1	G	E	R	U	N	D	A	T	O	P
2	L	A	N	E	R	I	N	G	E	R
3	T	O	M	A	T	O	S	P	A	S
4	A	C	T	U	P	H	A	R	S	H
5	T	I	R	E	A	T	T	A	I	N
6	V	E	S	T	A	C	H	I	E	R
7	M	A	P	L	E	S	E	L	S	A
8	L	A	K	E	R	S	K	I	C	K
9	W	I	N	E	L	I	N	G	E	R

68: Alphabet Soup

	N	A	P	K	I	N		
		U	M	B	R	E	L	L	A
		C	R	Y	S	T	A	L
B	O	U	T	I	Q	U	E
		D	E	V	E	L	O	P
		G	R	A	F	F	I	T	I
P	O	R	C	U	P	I	N	E
		O	X	Y	G	E	N
A	U	T	O	G	R	A	P	H
		A	D	J	A	C	E	N	T
	S	E	A	W	E	E	D
C	H	E	M	I	C	A	L
		M	I	X	T	U	R	E
	E	Y	E	L	A	S	H
M	A	S	Q	U	E	R	A	D	E
		S	P	O	N	G	E
W	E	A	T	H	E	R
		P	A	R	A	D	I	S	E
	B	A	L	A	N	C	E
	C	O	N	T	R	A	C	T
		D	O	M	I	N	O
M	A	G	A	Z	I	N	E
	A	C	C	I	D	E	N	T
S	C	H	E	D	U	L	E
		M	E	D	I	U	M
V	O	L	U	N	T	E	E	R

69: Contain Yourself

Frothy foam used with a razor (2 words) = <u>SHAVING CREAM</u>

One who loves his country = PA<u>TRIO</u>T

"Danger! Proceed with caution!" = BE<u>WAR</u>E

Beauty contests = P<u>AGE</u>ANTS

"There's nothing to do around here" feeling = BO<u>RED</u>OM

Bravery = C<u>OUR</u>AGE

One-wheeled ride = UN<u>ICY</u>CLE

Bad guy = VI<u>LLA</u>IN

Green stuff in the ocean = SE<u>AWE</u>ED

Small metric unit of length = CEN<u>TIME</u>TER

Vision = E<u>YES</u>IGHT

He knows what you're thinking (2 words) = MIN<u>D READ</u>ER

Do (an activity) regularly so as to improve at it = PR<u>ACTI</u>CE

Fudgy, cake-like dessert = BR<u>OWNI</u>E

70: You Can Quote Me

A. BATHTUB
B. BEEHIVE
C. FAKE
D. FIFTEEN
E. HAIKU
F. INITIAL
G. KNIGHT
H. MOUNTAIN
I. NOWHERE
J. OUTDOORS
K. RAINBOW
L. SILVER LINING
M. SWOON
N. TUTU
O. WIMPY
P. WISHBONE

"When I am working on a problem, I never think about beauty. But when I have finished, if the solution is not beautiful, I know it is wrong."—R. Buckminster Fuller

71: Cross-O

SCHOOL SUBJECTS: algebra, English, history, music, science

THINGS WITH BUTTONS: belly, calculator, elevator, microwave, shirt

VEGETABLES: artichoke, broccoli, carrot, spinach, turnip

THINGS YOU THROW: baseball, boomerang, Frisbee, javelin, tantrum

PUZZLES: crossword, jigsaw, Rubik's Cube, sudoku, word search

DOG BREEDS: beagle, boxer, Chihuahua, dachshund, Great Dane

72: One Two Three

C	LA	MOR					NO	CAN	DO
AGE	ND	A					STR	ES	SES
		LE	AP		JA	IL			
		PE	TER	PAN					
		TI	M	ES					
		PLA	TE		E	GO			
FA	STE	ST				SPE	N	T	
DE	AL	ER				L	ESS	ON	

73: Around the Bend

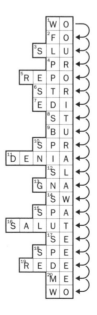

	W	O	
	2 F	O	
3 S	L	U	
	4 P	R	O
5 R	E	P	O
	6 S	T	R
	7 E	D	I
	8 S	T	
	9 B	U	
10 S	P	R	
11 D	E	N	I	A
	12 S	L	
13 G	N	A	
	14 S	W	
15 S	P	A	
16 S	A	L	U	T
	17 S	E	
	18 S	P	E
19 R	E	D	E
	20 M	E	
	W	O	

74: Trail Mix

A	C	A	R	E	H	E	L	E	N
B	C	A	P	E	S	L	I	N	G
C	E	M	U	C	A	U	G	H	T
D	S	E	D	A	N	V	I	N	E
E	A	R	M	O	R	A	S	K	S
F	G	N	A	T	E	L	E	C	T
G	E	V	E	N	T	R	E	A	L

75: Rows Garden

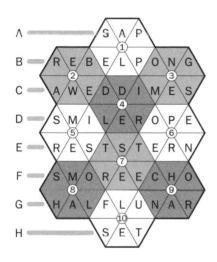

A — SAP
B — REBEL PONG
C — AWED DIMES
D — SMILE ROPE
E — REST STERN
F — SMORE ECHO
G — HALF LUNAR
H — SET

76: Circular Reasoning

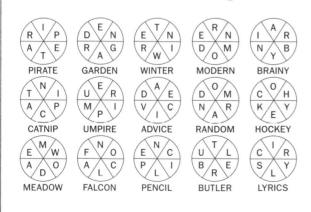

PIRATE	GARDEN	WINTER	MODERN	BRAINY
CATNIP	UMPIRE	ADVICE	RANDOM	HOCKEY
MEADOW	FALCON	PENCIL	BUTLER	LYRICS

77: Pyramid Scheme

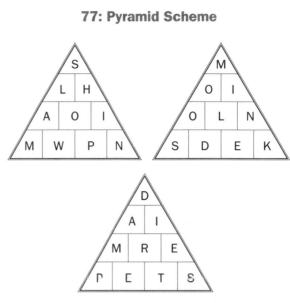

Each grid can be flipped horizontally and still be correct.

78: Flower Power

79: Triple Play

B	E	S	T	F	R	I	E	N	D
D	I	C	T	I	O	N	A	R	Y
P	R	I	N	C	I	P	A	L	S
G	R	E	A	T	L	A	K	E	S
C	E	N	T	I	M	E	T	E	R
M	I	C	R	O	S	C	O	P	E
O	C	E	A	N	L	I	N	E	R

W	H	I	T	E	B	R	E	A	D
I	N	N	O	V	A	T	I	V	E
S	C	U	L	P	T	U	R	E	S
C	R	E	D	I	T	C	A	R	D
P	O	L	I	T	I	C	I	A	N
F	A	I	R	E	N	O	U	G	H
V	I	D	E	O	G	A	M	E	S

81: To and Fro

N	G	I	S	B	I	T	E
O	R	N	I	L	O	I	V
S	A	S	N	A	K	R	A
A	M	P	S	S	E	E	S
E	B	E	A	T	S	M	E
R	E	C	E	I	P	T	D
M	G	T	L	S	I	R	I
E	Y	E	S	L	L	U	B
S	P	R	I	H	C	S	L
S	T	N	A	P	E	T	E

80: Strike One

1. EASTER BUNNY
2. TELEVISION
3. POWER DRILL
4. MICROPHONE
5. VOCAL CORDS
6. SALT SHAKER
7. BATHING SUIT
8. WHEELCHAIR
9. SOAP OPERA
10. BAKED POTATO
11. FINGER PAINTS
12. COFFEE TABLE
13. LEPRECHAUN
14. FIRST COUSIN

82: Riddle in the Middle

E	N	C	O	R	E	S
L	O	N	G	E	S	T
C	H	A	R	I	T	Y
P	A	T	I	E	N	T
L	U	L	L	A	B	Y
T	H	E	A	T	E	R
R	A	V	I	O	L	I
M	O	N	S	T	E	R

CONGA-RATULATIONS

G	R	A	N	I	T	E
I	L	L	E	G	A	L
S	T	R	O	B	E	S
C	A	P	T	U	R	E
T	I	N	I	E	S	T
I	C	E	L	A	N	D
P	R	O	F	I	L	E
S	C	A	L	P	E	L
W	E	A	K	E	S	T

IT'LL BE A PIECE OF CAKE

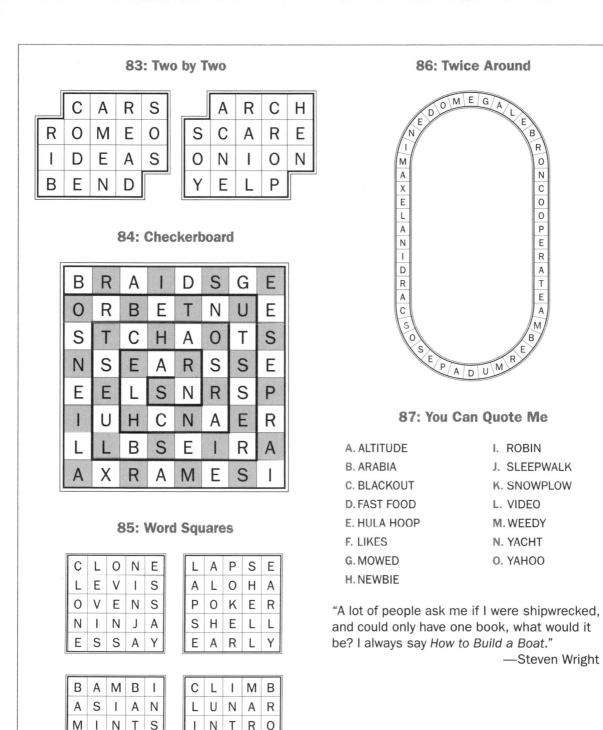

83: Two by Two

```
C A R S
R O M E O
I D E A S
B E N D
```

```
A R C H
S C A R E
O N I O N
Y E L P
```

84: Checkerboard

```
B R A I D S G E
O R B E T N U E
S T C H A O T S
N S E A R S S E
E E L S N R S P
I U H C N A E R
L L B S E I R A
A X R A M E S I
```

85: Word Squares

```
C L O N E
L E V I S
O V E N S
N I N J A
E S S A Y
```

```
L A P S E
A L O H A
P O K E R
S H E L L
E A R L Y
```

```
B A M B I
A S I A N
M I N T S
B A T H E
I N S E T
```

```
C L I M B
L U N A R
I N T R O
M A R I O
B R O O M
```

86: Twice Around

87: You Can Quote Me

A. ALTITUDE
B. ARABIA
C. BLACKOUT
D. FAST FOOD
E. HULA HOOP
F. LIKES
G. MOWED
H. NEWBIE
I. ROBIN
J. SLEEPWALK
K. SNOWPLOW
L. VIDEO
M. WEEDY
N. YACHT
O. YAHOO

"A lot of people ask me if I were shipwrecked, and could only have one book, what would it be? I always say *How to Build a Boat*."
—Steven Wright

88: Zebra Crossing

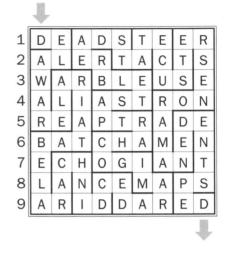

Grid (rows 1–3):
- 1: G R O M A T O N E C A L M
- 2: B E S T I D E M I T E N
- 3: S E L E C T N O O P A L

89 : Gotta Split

P	E	N	N	Y				R	E	S	T	S
A		E		A	N	K	L	E		T		L
J	A	P	A	N		I		C	A	R	G	O
A		T		K	E	N	Y	A		A		W
M	O	U	S	E		G		L	A	N	C	E
A		N		E	A	S	E	L		G		S
S	L	E	D	S				S	W	E	A	T

90: Shapeshifters

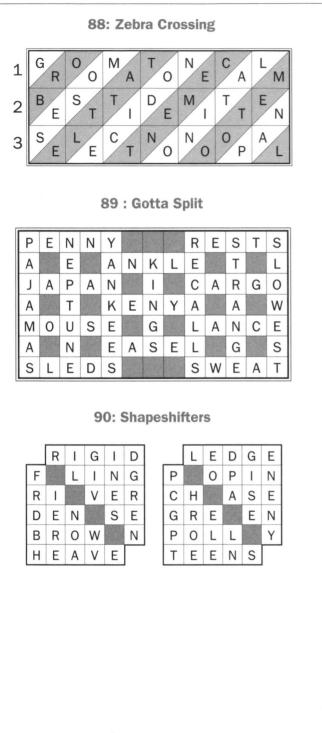

Left grid:
- R I G I D
- F L I N G
- R I V E R
- D E N S E
- B R O W N
- H E A V E

Right grid:
- L E D G E
- P O P I N
- C H A S E
- G R E E N
- P O L L Y
- T E E N S

91: Labyrinth

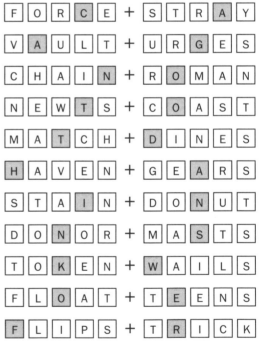

	1	D E A D S T E E R
	2	A L E R T A C T S
	3	W A R B L E U S E
	4	A L I A S T R O N
	5	R E A P T R A D E
	6	B A T C H A M E N
	7	E C H O G I A N T
	8	L A N C E M A P S
	9	A R I D D A R E D

92: Knockouts

FORCE + STRAY
VAULT + URGES
CHAIN + ROMAN
NEWTS + COAST
MATCH + DINES
HAVEN + GEARS
STAIN + DONUT
DONOR + MASTS
TOKEN + WAILS
FLOAT + TEENS
FLIPS + TRICK

"Silence is golden when you can't think of a good answer."

93: Hexed

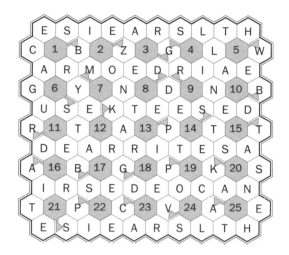

E	S	I	E	A	R	S	L	T	H

C 1 B 2 Z 3 G 4 L 5 W
A R M O E D R I A E
G 6 Y 7 N 8 D 9 N 10 B
U S E K T E E S E D
R 11 T 12 A 13 P 14 T 15 T
D E A R R I T E S A
A 16 B 17 G 18 P 19 K 20 S
I R S E D E O C A N
T 21 P 22 C 23 V 24 A 25 E
E S I E A R S L T H

94: One Two Three

F	RO	LIC				CHA	PL	IN
UN	SE	EN				R	OW	DY
		SE	VEN		WA	GES		
			GE	TI	T			
			FU	LL	FR			
		HAI	L		SKI	P		
CU	STA	RD				RE	CLU	SE
TE	MP	O				STO	CK	ED

95: Bits and Pieces

LEG	S	GENTLEST
TENT	O	ANTIDOTE
AID	M	DIAGRAMS
RAGS	E	SHORTAGE
HOT	S	TROPHIES
RIPE	C	PRACTICE
ACT	R	FRACTION
INFO	A	FOUNTAIN
NUT	M	TANTRUMS
RATS	B	SUBTRACT
CUT	L	CURLIEST
RISE	E	INCREASE
CAN	D	SANDWICH
WISH	E	SIDESHOW
SOD	G	ROAD SIGN
RAIN	G	RELAXING
LEX	S	EXPLORES
ROPE		

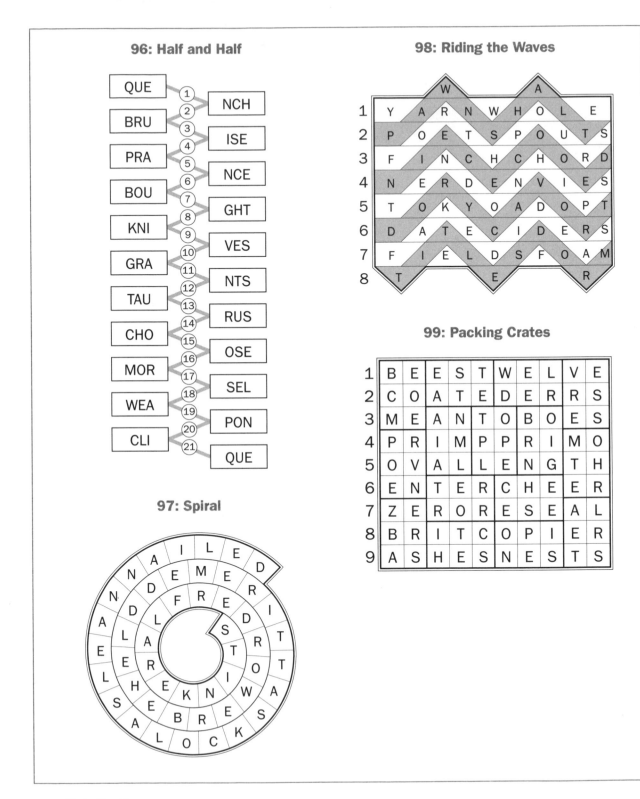

96: Half and Half

Left: QUE, BRU, PRA, BOU, KNI, GRA, TAU, CHO, MOR, WEA, CLI

(circles numbered 1–21)

Right: NCH, ISE, NCE, GHT, VES, NTS, RUS, OSE, SEL, PON, QUE

98: Riding the Waves

		W				A			
1	Y	A	R	N	W	H	O	L	E
2	P	O	E	T	S	P	O	U	T S
3	F	I	N	C	H	C	H	O	R D
4	N	E	R	D	E	N	V	I	E S
5	T	O	K	Y	O	A	D	O	P T
6	D	A	T	E	C	I	D	E	R S
7	F	I	E	L	D	S	F	O	A M
8	T				E				R

99: Packing Crates

1	B	E	E	S	T	W	E	L	V E
2	C	O	A	T	E	D	E	R	R S
3	M	E	A	N	T	O	B	O	E S
4	P	R	I	M	P	P	R	I	M O
5	O	V	A	L	L	E	N	G	T H
6	E	N	T	E	R	C	H	E	E R
7	Z	E	R	O	R	E	S	E	A L
8	B	R	I	T	C	O	P	I	E R
9	A	S	H	E	S	N	E	S	T S

97: Spiral

100: Wordplay City

- ▶ SAN DIEGO
- ▶ DALLAS (SALAD)
- ▶ COLUMBUS
- ▶ INDIANAPOLIS (DIANA)
- ▶ FORT WORTH (TWO)
- ▶ TUCSON
- ▶ AUSTIN (BOSTON)
- ▶ BALTIMORE
- ▶ CLEVELAND (LEVEL)
- ▶ HONOLULU
- ▶ SEATTLE (CATTLE)
- ▶ SAN JOSE (BANJO)
- ▶ WASHINGTON
- ▶ DENVER (DEER)

The first letters of the remaining
answers spell the word
AIRPLANE.

102: Games Cabinet

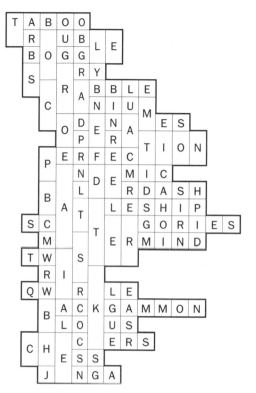

101: Mental Blocks

103: Cross-O

SEA CREATURES: dolphin, lobster, octopus, shrimp,
   whale

SPORTS: badminton, hockey, lacrosse, squash,
   tennis

SCHOOL SUPPLIES: backpack, calculator, notebook,
   pencil, ruler

PARTS OF A CAR: battery, dashboard, engine, fender,
   windshield

TREES: cedar, maple, redwood, spruce, willow

THINGS WITH WHEELS: ambulance, motorcycle,
   stroller, tractor, wagon

104: For Starters

	B	C	S	G
F	R	O	T	H
R	O	M	E	O
J	A	M	E	S
A	D	A	P	T

	Z	W	H	P
E	E	R	I	E
T	R	I	K	E
V	O	T	E	R
U	S	E	R	S

105: Triple Play

G	I	V	E	O	R	T	A	K	E
E	V	I	L	G	E	N	I	U	S
F	O	R	E	X	A	M	P	L	E
S	A	T	E	L	L	I	T	E	S
B	L	U	E	R	I	B	B	O	N
D	R	A	W	S	T	R	I	N	G
V	O	L	L	E	Y	B	A	L	L

S	P	E	E	D	D	E	M	O	N
G	O	O	S	E	B	U	M	P	S
O	P	T	I	M	I	S	T	I	C
H	U	M	A	N	B	E	I	N	G
C	L	O	T	H	E	S	P	I	N
W	A	F	F	L	E	I	R	O	N
T	R	A	M	P	O	L	I	N	E

106: Rows Garden

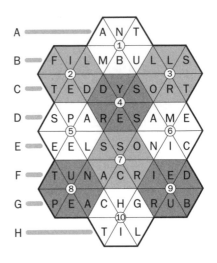

107: Pinwheel

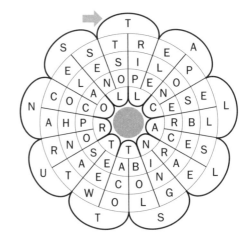

108: To and Fro

M	A	L	E	P	A	N	E
A	U	E	G	A	R	A	G
E	T	A	C	I	L	E	D
R	O	P	E	N	S	C	E
C	E	D	I	T	W	O	L
S	E	A	F	O	O	D	I
K	T	Y	U	E	L	M	S
C	O	I	N	S	L	O	T
E	R	O	N	G	I	T	E
N	W	A	Y	S	P	A	N

109: Word Squares

S	C	R	A	M
C	R	A	T	E
R	A	I	L	S
A	T	L	A	S
M	E	S	S	Y

C	A	N	A	L
A	R	O	M	A
N	O	W	A	Y
A	M	A	Z	E
L	A	Y	E	R

J	A	B	B	A
A	R	I	E	L
B	I	N	G	O
B	E	G	I	N
A	L	O	N	E

V	E	R	B	S
E	M	A	I	L
R	A	I	N	Y
B	I	N	G	E
S	L	Y	E	R

110: A Little Something Extra

1 BREAD + V = ADVERB
2 NACHO + R = ANCHOR
3 BUTANE + Q = BANQUET
4 BINGO + X = BOXING
5 CATNAP + I = CAPTAIN
6 RECAP + T = CARPET
7 CHAIRS + E = CASHIER
8 ACORN + Y = CRAYON
9 TORQUE + A = EQUATOR
10 FATES + N = FASTEN
11 REHEAT + F = FEATHER
12 LODGER + W = GROWLED
13 CUTIES + J = JUSTICE
14 MAIL FR + C = MIRACLE
15 CLAIMS + U = MUSICAL
16 RENOWN + B = NEWBORN
17 APRON + D = PARDON
18 OPINE + G = PIGEON
19 LEGIT + P = PIGLET
20 BUMPER + L = PLUMBER
21 RINSE + O = SENIOR
22 PILES + M = SIMPLE
23 PEARLS + K = SPARKLE
24 MASCOT + H = STOMACH
25 TUNES + S = SUNSET
26 COPIED + Z = ZIP CODE